Understanding
Matthew

The Early Christian Worldview
of the First Gospel

Stephen Westerholm

Baker Academic
Grand Rapids, Michigan

© 2006 by Stephen Westerholm

Published by Baker Academic
a division of Baker Publishing Group
P.O. Box 6287, Grand Rapids, MI 49516-6287
www.bakeracademic.com

Printed in the United States of America

Library of Congress Cataloging-in-Publication Data
Westerholm, Stephen, 1949–
    Understanding Matthew : the early Christian worldview of the First
  Gospel / Stephen Westerholm.
        p.   cm.
    Includes bibliographical references and index.
    ISBN 10: 0-8010-2738-1 (pbk.)
    ISBN 978-0-8010-2738-3 (pbk.)
    1. Bible. N.T. Matthew—Criticism, interpretation, etc. I. Title.
  BS2575.52.W47 2006
  226.2′06—dc22   2005031721

For Dr. Gerald B. Griffiths and "Mrs. G.,"
with whom I studied the stories of Jesus

Contents

Introduction

In the German election of November 1932, the National Socialist (Nazi) Party of Adolf Hitler received 33 percent of the popular vote and thus became the largest party in the German Reichstag (or Parliament). The prospect of a country run by Hitler filled many people with alarm, and various alternative proposals for forming a government were tried. Each failed, however, and in the end, in the misbegotten belief that Hitler could be controlled if given a share in power, the Nazi Party leader was invited to become chancellor on January 30, 1933.

Hitler was not to be controlled; within half a year he had destroyed the fledgling German democracy. A fire conveniently set to the Reichstag became his excuse for suspending ("temporarily") individual rights on February 28. On March 23 he effectively (though not officially) abolished the Weimar Constitution, transferring power from the Reichstag to the Nazi administration. In May the Nazis replaced the labor unions with a state-controlled labor front. All political parties except that of the Nazis were disbanded in June; in July they were declared illegal. The dictatorship was firmly in place that for a dozen years would run—as it ruined—Germany and inflict on the world the catastrophe of a world war and the horrors of the Holocaust.

Nor were the churches of Germany left to themselves. Promising to reconstruct the nation on a Christian foundation, the

Nazis attempted to unite all the Protestant churches in a single national church under a national bishop (the Nazi Ludwig Müller). That the "Christianity" of the Nazis had a distinctly German flavor was only to be expected: if religion (as the Nazis believed) has its roots in a country's "soul" and its people's "blood," it seemed to follow that German Christianity should be characterized by German ideals of heroism and strength. It was also important to preserve the "purity" of German Christendom: non-"Aryans" must have no part in its ministry. Many Germans—including many church leaders—were only too willing to comply.

In addition to *Discipleship*, Dietrich Bonhoeffer (1906–1945) published several other books during his lifetime, of which the most famous is *Life Together*.[1] Important publications after his death include *Letters and Papers from Prison* and the fragmentary *Ethics*.[2] Today he is best known, however, for his opposition to the Nazis and his death at their hands.

Out of the German church struggle of the 1930s, at least one modern spiritual classic emerged: Dietrich Bonhoeffer's *Discipleship*.[3] The young Bonhoeffer ran a seminary for preachers that was set up by the dissenting ("Confessing") churches from early 1935 until the Gestapo shut it down in the fall of 1937. The book, published shortly after the closing of the seminary, was based on a series of lectures that Bonhoeffer had given to his students. Its topic: what does it mean to be a disciple of Jesus Christ?

The question is presumably of concern to Christians in every age; but it took on extraordinary urgency in the Germany of the 1930s, when opposition to the idolatry, racism, and ruthlessness of the Nazis was savagely suppressed. (Bonhoeffer himself was executed by the Nazis, after a two-year imprisonment, in April 1945—less than a month before Hitler committed suicide and the

---

1. Dietrich Bonhoeffer, *Life Together; Prayerbook of the Bible* (Minneapolis: Fortress, 1996).

2. Dietrich Bonhoeffer, *Letters and Papers from Prison*, ed. Eberhard Bethge, expanded ed. (New York: Simon & Schuster, 1997); and *Ethics* (Minneapolis: Fortress, 2005).

3. Dietrich Bonhoeffer, *Discipleship*, trans. B. Green and R. Krauss (Minneapolis: Fortress, 2001). Originally published in German as *Nachfolge* (Munich: Christian Kaiser, 1937). The original English translation was *The Cost of Discipleship*, trans. R. H. Fuller, abridged trans. (London: SCM; New York: Macmillan, 1949).

Allies celebrated victory in Europe.) The answer, for Bonhoeffer, was scarcely to be sought in the slogans of warring parties in the church. The "sole concern" of the disciple of Jesus must rather be with what Jesus himself wanted to say: "We want to know what Jesus wants."[4] Yet discovering what Jesus wants is itself no easy matter. Over the centuries Jesus' words have been overlaid by "harsh laws" and "false hopes," by incomprehensible sermons, human institutions, and doctrine. If we are to hear the "call of Jesus" today, we must "be led back to scripture, to the word and call of Jesus Christ himself."[5] Bonhoeffer's *Discipleship* is largely a commentary on sayings of Jesus from the Gospel of Matthew, particularly from the Sermon on the Mount (Matthew 5–7).

Bonhoeffer was concerned not only to understand but also to practice the kind of discipleship prescribed in Matthew's Gospel; as a result, there is much in his story to illuminate the study of Matthew. Still, our primary goal here is to understand the Gospel itself; and with this goal in mind, it is perhaps worthwhile to stress at the outset that Bonhoeffer's approach is only *one* of the ways in which the Gospel can profitably be read.

The Gospel of Matthew was likely written during the last quarter of the first century of our era. Its place of origin is less certain: the city of Antioch in Syria is a common, and educated, guess. A book written in first-century Antioch will inevitably differ from one written in fifth-century Rome, or twelfth-century Paris, or twentieth-century Germany, even if the subject matter is the same: each will reflect, in a variety of ways, the conditions under which it was written. It follows that the Gospel of Matthew is of interest not only to would-be disciples of Jesus (such as Bonhoeffer) but also to scholars interested in the historical setting in which the author wrote.[6] Students of ancient history, or of the origins of Christianity, or of early Christian relations with Jews will all want to search Matthew for evidence to illuminate their fields of inquiry. Others, fascinated to learn what people ate in the first century, what clothes they wore, or how

4. Bonhoeffer, *Discipleship* (2001), 37.
5. Ibid., 37–38.
6. Traditionally the Gospel writer has been identified as Matthew, one of Jesus' twelve disciples. Scholars today still find it convenient to speak of the author as "Matthew" though recognizing that the Gospel itself is anonymous and that its writer can no longer be identified.

they lived, will naturally look for details in the Gospel that reflect the realities of everyday life. Taking a step back from the
content of the Gospel, we may note that Matthew was written
in first-century Greek; students of the language have their own
legitimate interest in Matthew's writing. Moreover, since what
Matthew wrote is a story, students interested in narrative literature—in the structure of a story, for example, or how its plot and
characters are developed—will read the Gospel with these topics
in mind. Students of anthropology and sociology will attempt to
illuminate aspects of the Gospel with the explanatory models of
their disciplines. In short, the ways in which Matthew's Gospel
can be, and has been, read are endless.

Some students, confronted with these more or less academic
approaches to the Gospel (or to the Bible in general) become
impatient, insisting that "that's *not* what the Gospel (or the Bible)
is really about." They have a point, of course; but their point is
scarcely a decisive objection to the kinds of reading mentioned
above, and it may even rest on a misunderstanding. To be sure,
the Gospel of Matthew is (to use an ambiguous but useful term) a
"religious" book, and students for whom it is sacred scripture may
well be frustrated by readings of the Gospel that appear impervi-
ous to its religious dimension. Certainly, no serious reader of the
Gospel can fail to observe that the Gospel sees our world as God's
world and interprets human possibilities and responsibilities
in the light of this conviction. But precisely because Matthew's
Gospel is concerned with how life is to be lived in *this* world, it
uses ordinary human language to speak of ordinary human beings who (like all human beings) lived in a society where there
were conventional ways of eating, drinking, and doing one's daily
business. Not only must we say that the study of these dimensions of the text is a legitimate academic pursuit; the awareness
that religious beliefs and practices take shape in history and are
part of human culture is essential to a mature understanding
of religion—including Christianity and the Gospel of Matthew.
(Indeed, Christian faith itself sees God at work in the processes
of history and the development of human culture.)

The focus of the kinds of reading mentioned above is in each
case determined by interests that the reader brings to the text.
The *writer* of the Gospel had no intention of informing us about
first-century language, customs, or culture; nor would he have

recognized the social-scientific language with which contemporary scholars explain aspects of his text. That he had very different purposes for writing by no means prevents us from reading what he wrote to find evidence relevant to our own inquiries. From such readings we may, however, distinguish a second type of approach to the Gospel, one that allows the text itself to set the agenda. Legitimate and useful though it may be, in certain contexts, to attend only to those aspects of another's words that relate to our questions, one can only hope that not *all* our relations with other human beings are so narrowly focused. Some relationships require us to give as well as take. Friends (among whom we may include spouses) count on us to listen to what *they* are saying when they speak to us; teachers and bosses entertain similar expectations. Nor, ideally, is our readiness to listen limited to the circle of those with whom we immediately interact: we expand our mental horizons when we are prepared to expose our minds to the thinking of those whose views diverge significantly from our own. Our ability to relate to others, our own growth as human beings, and the breadth of our understanding of the world in which we live all depend on our willingness to listen to others.

> The awareness that religious beliefs and practices take shape in history and are part of human culture is essential to a mature understanding of religion—and of the Gospel of Matthew.

The importance of listening to others applies equally whether we are in their presence and can hear them speak or are removed from their presence and can only read what they have written. Indeed, often people write for no other reason than that they are unable to speak directly to their readers. In writing "I love you!" or "Please bring me some Swiss chocolates when you return" or "I've never been so exhausted in all my life!" they mean exactly what they would have meant if they had spoken the same words. Of course, we cannot always take words at their face value. If we want to get along with others, we normally have to take them at their word and believe that they mean what they say (or write) and that they say (or write) what they mean. (Have you ever tried to carry on an ordinary conversation with psychoanalysts who refuse to leave their work at the office?) But at times we all use words to say something different from what our words by themselves might appear to mean. "I love you!" may really mean "Please bring me some Swiss chocolates when you return." Conversely, "Please bring me some Swiss chocolates when you return" may mean "Do you love me?" And "I've never been so exhausted in all my life!" may really mean "Don't even think to ask me to move your books again!" But again, words that signal a message different from their surface meaning may be either spoken or written.

One obvious *difference* between the two ways of communicating a message is that written words must themselves suffice to convey what their writer wants to say whereas speakers can reinforce their point with their tone of voice or an accompanying gesture. Moreover, we can often question people who speak to us and have them clear up what we find obscure in their words; writers are seldom so accessible. On the other hand, writing has its own advantages. Generally we choose our words more carefully when we write them. And usually we can revise what we write before it reaches others, whereas words that once escape the barrier of our teeth can never be recalled.

> Our ability to relate to others, our own growth as human beings, and the breadth of our understanding of the world in which we live all depend on our willingness to listen to others.

If it is true that both speaking and writing have advantages and disadvantages for communicating a message, then it is also the case that not all attempts at communication succeed. When they do not, the fault may lie either with the source of the communication (the one who speaks or writes) or with the recipient (those who hear or read).[7] The former may be guilty of poor formulation, of failing to choose the right words to communicate the intended message. In such cases, recipients generally attempt to figure out as best they can what the source of the message meant to say. (Teachers frequently find themselves in this situation when reading students' essays. Students frequently find themselves in this situation when reading teachers' exami-

---

7. We may ignore here the further possibility that messages may become corrupted after they have left their source and before they reach their recipient: poor messengers (or sound systems!) may distort a spoken message; poor copying or editing may distort a written message that passes through the hands of a third party.

nation questions.) Alternatively, the recipient of the message, whether spoken or written, may be too dull, too inattentive, or too uninformed to grasp the intended meaning. Whatever their cause, the problems that at times arise in our attempts to communicate highlight several obvious but important points. We use words when we want to communicate. We choose words that we believe will convey what we want to communicate. People who hear or read the words of others normally assume that the words mean what the speaker or writer meant them to mean. When words are well chosen and intelligently received, they serve the purpose of communicating a message from their source to their recipient.

If the first type of reader mentioned above reads the words of another to answer his or her own questions, the second type reads to learn what another has to say, to grasp the message that the writer intended to communicate. The latter task is often simple enough. When the communication is mundane ("Please bring me some Swiss chocolates"), we generally grasp what is written without further reflection. But complex texts, especially those from a culture very different from our own, can only be understood if we make some effort to enter their authors' way of thinking, to see things the way their authors did. This is the justification for books (such as this one) intended to facilitate a modern reader's understanding of an ancient, and significant, text.

> If one type of reader reads the words of another to answer his or her own questions, a second type reads to learn what another has to say.

Some texts present difficulties of another sort for readers intent on learning what they have to say. When someone writes in order to inform, persuade, or make a request, we say that we have grasped the text's meaning when we understand the information that the writer intended to convey, the argument with which the writer intended to convince, the request that the writer intended to make. But what is the meaning of a narrative or poetic text? Stories and poems are not easily reduced to a single message. They are hardly ideal media for anyone who simply wants to inform, persuade, or request; yet they are much better suited than straightforward statements for helping us *see* things differently than we normally would. If story writers or poets intend to convey a message through what they write, then it must be said that the intended message does not exhaust the meaning of the composition (unless it is a very poor composition indeed). Good stories and poems take on a life of their own, affect different readers in different ways, and carry new meaning as they are read in new situations.

The Gospel of Matthew is clearly a text of the latter sort. Not only is the Gospel itself a story; a number of stories (the parables) are told within the main story, and both the main story and the stories it contains have proven inexhaustible in the meanings they carry. That being said, it is also true that the writer of the Gospel gave it its present shape and included in the Gospel its present contents precisely because there was information that he wanted his readers to know, truth of which he wanted to persuade them, behavior that he wanted them to adopt. As a result, although Matthew has written an inexhaustible text, readers from the first century until our own have derived the same basic message from his Gospel: Jesus (Matthew wants us to know) is a fit object of devotion and discipleship. The details of the Gospel, as all attentive readers sense, are meant to spell out why this is true about Jesus and what discipleship of Jesus entails. If we read Matthew's text to learn what it has to say rather than merely as a springboard for our own speculations, then even the new meanings that we find in the Gospel should bear some discernible relation to this basic message: because Jesus is who the Gospel says he is, he is to be followed in the way the Gospel prescribes.

The present study is meant rather as a preface to the second kind of reading than as an example of how such reading may be done. The goal is to assist readers to whom the world of Matthew is foreign (and this, in varying degrees, is true of all of us) to make sense of the Gospel when they read it. Given the nature of the Gospel, the themes we look at will inevitably involve the foundational human questions that we label "religious": what is the nature of our world, how ought we to live, where are we headed, and the like. If we are to see the world as Matthew sees it and understand the message of his text, then clearly these are the types of questions we will need to consider. And to be sure, it is primarily through its answers to such questions that the

Gospel has influenced its readers for many centuries. However intriguing the Gospel of Matthew may prove for linguists, social scientists, and historians of antiquity, and however legitimate their inquiries may be, the main importance of the Gospel throughout its history lies in the way that it has shaped the lives of millions of readers attuned to its message. To understand the Gospel of Matthew is a prerequisite for understanding much that has happened in the past and much that we encounter in our world today.

Finally, it must simply be conceded that even a reading of the Gospel whose goal is to understand what it has to say differs *essentially* from Bonhoeffer's reading of the same text—and, moreover, that Bonhoeffer was the kind of reader that Matthew desired. My own academic work has been devoted primarily to the study and teaching of early Christianity; at times, however, I have been called upon to introduce students to Judaism and Islam as well. In each case I make it a goal to enable students, mainly through the reading of texts significant within each tradition, to see how the world looks through Jewish or Christian or Muslim eyes. Such a goal can never be fully achieved; but to the extent that it can be approximated, I believe that students are better able to relate to others, grow themselves as human beings, and have a broader understanding of the world in which they live. These, it seems to me, are worthy objectives. It remains true, however, that to read the scriptures of Jews, Christians, or Muslims with these goals in mind is very different from reading them *as* a Jew or Christian or Muslim. In the end, religions are meant to be lived, not merely discussed, compared, or even "understood." The difference is that between mastering alternative views of child psychology and actually raising a child; between investigating the benefits to be derived from swimming and actually diving into the water; between observing adolescent behavior and actually falling in love; between lecturing on gerontology and experiencing what it *means* to grow old. Matthew wrote, as Bonhoeffer wrote, not to inform readers of the nature of Christian discipleship but to summon them to a *life* of discipleship. Readers who fail to note the difference, whatever their grasp of Matthean themes, will have fundamentally misunderstood the Gospel.

1

Of Worldviews
and Perspectives

You know the plot. Bad guy captures good guy. Bad guy gloats, believing he has good guy in his power and can annihilate him. Good guy shows no fear, knowing that (a) escape is easily managed, or (b) he can overcome bad guy with his secret weapon, or (c) help is on the way and will arrive in the nick of time. Bad guy knows nothing of (a), (b), or (c). The tables are turned, bad guy is confounded (and perhaps annihilated), good guy triumphs. . . . Such is the basic story. Names and places, gender and number, weapons and ways of escape, plausibility and story-telling skill all vary. But the basic plot is the stuff of countless novels, TV shows, movies, and more than a few stories in the Bible.

In the biblical versions of the story, the unseen resource on which good guys rely is always God. Bad guys who believe that good guys are in their power fail to realize that it is nothing for God to deliver his faithful associates from besieging armies, the flames of a furnace, the mouths of lions, threatening mobs, prisons, or executioners. Good guys know that God rules and is ready to give help when counted on to do so.

The same point is asserted outright in many of the hymns and prayers that make up the book of Psalms in the Bible. When the psalm writer praises God with the words "Your kingdom is an everlasting kingdom, and your dominion endures throughout all generations,"[1] he simply means that God rules at all times, that God is always in control. "[God's] kingdom rules over all," another psalm writer assures us,[2] making the point that God's rule is universal as well as eternal. The news provides reassurance, of course, only if accompanied by the convictions that God is kind and good, on the one hand, and dependable in providing aid, on the other. On both these counts as well, the psalm writers speak with confidence:

> The LORD is good to all,
>   and his compassion is over all that he has made. . . .
> The LORD is near to all who call on him,
>   to all who call on him in truth.
> He fulfills the desire of all who fear him;
>   he also hears their cry, and saves them.[3]

The God who rules everywhere and at all times is also just. If self-seeking, dishonest, violent people (bad guys, in other words) seem to succeed in the world, we can be sure that their prosperity will be short-lived.

> I have seen the wicked oppressing,
>   and towering like a cedar of Lebanon.
> Again I passed by, and they were no more;
>   though I sought them, they could not be found.[4]

Conversely, good people who suffer can expect God's deliverance.

> Many are the afflictions of the righteous,
>   but the LORD rescues them from them all.[5]

1. Psalm 145:13.
2. Psalm 103:19.
3. Psalm 145:9, 18–19.
4. Psalm 37:35–36.
5. Psalm 34:19.

Why should bad people prosper at all, or good people ever suffer? Even subjects of a divine king sometimes choose to ignore or flout his rule; whenever they do, trouble and chaos are bound to result. When, on the other hand, God sees fit to intervene, he will put things right—otherwise he would not be just. The earth and all its inhabitants who love peace and justice can rejoice in the assurance that God puts things right in the world.

> According to the book of Psalms in the Bible, the earth and all its inhabitants who love peace and justice can rejoice in the assurance that God puts things right in the world.

> Let the heavens be glad, and let the earth rejoice;
>   let the sea roar, and all that fills it;
>   let the field exult, and everything in it.
> Then shall all the trees of the forest sing for joy
>   before the LORD; for he is coming,
>   for he is coming to judge the earth.
> He will judge the world with righteousness,
>   and the peoples with his truth.[6]

Opposing Worldviews

Needless to say, the worldview that underlies the ancient stories and psalms in the Bible differs widely from the worldview of many who live in modern Western (and Eastern) society. It is easy to show, moreover, that in essential respects the worldview of these stories and psalms is taken for granted by the Jesus of Matthew's Gospel. But before we look specifically at Matthew, we would be wise to pause and consider what we mean by Matthew's (or anyone else's) worldview. Let me begin with an example of opposing worldviews; then, using the example as a starting point, I will make a few observations about my use of the term.

Barney and Bernie go for a walk in the woods. Barney sees the fields and trees, the butterflies and birds. He thinks it all very beautiful but sees no deeper significance in nature's beauty. Bernie sees the same beauty as the handiwork of God.

6. Psalm 96:11–13.

Barney and his wife, Beulah, have a baby. They are pleased, of course, but see nothing extraordinary in the event: sperm meets egg cell; sperm fertilizes egg cell; fertilized cell moves to uterus; in uterus cell cluster grows into embryo; embryo develops organs and limbs—and so on until the baby is born. Bernie and his wife, Bertha, have a baby as well. However often babies are born and however aware Bernie and Bertha may be of the way babies are conceived, grow in the womb, and come to birth, the happy couple cannot but see in the life and birth of their baby daughter a wonder—and a gift from God.

Barney and Beulah resolve to be good parents. Beyond the requirements of the law, they feel no obligation to do so; but looking at the various activities to which they might devote their time, they conclude that they value good parenting most. Bernie and Bertha believe they have a sacred obligation to care for the child with whom they have been entrusted. They can scarcely envisage themselves neglecting this obligation; they are sure, in any case, that it would be wrong for them to do so.

Confronted with Bernie's way of thinking, Barney believes that Bernie has projected his wishes onto the universe: having grown up in a warm family where all his needs were met, Bernie now imagines that the universe functions in the same way, with God playing the role of the caring, benevolent, duty-assigning parent. Apart from wishful thinking, Barney can see no reason to adopt Bernie's outlook on life. For his part, Bernie, confronted with Barney's way of thinking, thinks Barney to be shortsighted. In Bernie's mind, Barney fails to see, beyond fields and trees, the glory of their Creator; beyond the wonder of a baby's new life, the Giver of all life; beyond human values, the rights and wrongs among which we choose in a world that we inhabit but whose underlying order we did not shape.

Defining Worldviews

What, then, may we say about worldviews in the light of this example?

1. The same phenomena (the beauty of nature, the birth of a child, the task of a parent, and so forth) may be looked upon very differently, depending on the answers we give to certain

fundamental questions: whether life on earth is the product of chance or design; whether we have obligations to fulfill or simply shape our own values; and so on. Our answers to these basic questions about life itself provide the framework within which we understand the particular phenomena we encounter in the course of living. Just as we need to have some notion of what a sport or game is if we are to understand the particular phenomena we see at a football game, and just as we need to be aware of the big picture (in, for example, Leonardo da Vinci's *Last Supper*) that the artist is depicting if we are to understand details of the painting, so we need a rudimentary grasp of what life itself is about to make sense of individual incidents in our experience. Our basic understanding of life, the framework within which we interpret our lives and the world around us, we may call our worldview.

> Our basic understanding of life, the framework within which we interpret our lives and the world around us, we may call our worldview.

2. The term "perspective" is often used as an equivalent to "worldview": from Barney's *perspective*, good parenting is nothing more than a human choice or value; from Bernie's *perspective*, good parenting is a sacred obligation. But here a distinction should be kept in mind. The term "perspective" is generally used of the vantage point (whether literal or metaphorical) from which we view a particular phenomenon. Given that the same phenomenon may appear in quite different lights from different vantage points, we generally reckon with the possibility that different views, arrived at from different perspectives, may all be correct: from one perspective, a certain mountain is high; from another, not particularly. Indeed, a single individual can entertain different perspectives on the same phenomenon at the same time: from one perspective, Dave thinks that the devaluation of the dollar would be a good thing, though he recognizes that, from another perspective, it would not. A view advanced on the basis of a particular perspective presupposes that the same phenomenon can be viewed differently, from a different angle, with different, but not necessarily less true, results.

A worldview, on the other hand, is not advanced as one perspective on a particular phenomenon within the whole of reality but as a claim about the nature of reality itself. It is like a solution to a problem, although here the problem is the very nature of life: we can begin to make sense of a myriad of particular phenomena that we encounter in life once we recognize that a, b, and c are true about life itself. (For Barney, a = there is no God; b = we're on our own in the universe; c = we have to shape our own values. For Bernie, a = there is a God; b = all that is owes its existence to God; c = as parts of God's creation, human beings live within boundaries of right and wrong that they ought to respect.) It follows that although the same person may view a given phenomenon from different perspectives, no one person at one time can seriously hold differing worldviews. Some people (to take a common example) believe that there is a God who created us. Other people believe there is no such being, or have no decided view on the matter, or suspect that some power greater than humans exists but feel unable to say anything more. *No one*, however, can plausibly say, "From one perspective, there is a God; from another, there isn't!"[7]

> A worldview is not advanced as one perspective on a particular phenomenon within the whole of reality but as a claim about the nature of reality itself.

3. Although we need some sense of what life itself is about to make sense of particular phenomena, we can have no sense of what life is about apart from the experience of particular phenomena. To return to our football analogy: without a grasp of what a sport is, we can make no sense of the scene on a football field when a group of people run down someone carrying a ball, hit him viciously, then walk away as though nothing has happened. On the other hand, we can have no grasp of what a sport is unless we are familiar with the way in which particular games, such as football, are played. In the same way we develop our worldview—our basic interpretation of life—as life provides us with experiences that require interpretation. Moreover, the basic understanding we have of life is itself subject to change as we are exposed to new experiences: "conversions" of various kinds do take place, either because we become aware of alter-

---

7. Unless one means that some arguments suggest that there is a God whereas other arguments suggest that there is not. If this is what one means, there are better ways of saying it.

native worldviews that seem more satisfactory than our own or because we encounter phenomena for which our current worldview provides no satisfactory explanation.

4. It is possible to claim that one holds a particular worldview even though the way one speaks, the choices one makes, and the activities in which one engages fail to reflect that claim. Many people, for example, purport to believe in an existence beyond this life whose character (heaven or hell, reincarnation or liberation from the cycle of death and rebirth, and so forth) will be determined by how one lives here on earth; yet the choices they make are at times no different from those made by people who believe one should simply live for the moment. Are they hypocrites? That seems a harsh judgment. The simplest explanation is that human beings have always found it easiest to look no further ahead than at what will satisfy their immediate needs and desires. It takes concentration, discipline, and effort if we are to consider, before we choose, what action would best promote our well-being beyond this present life—and not even the firmest believer is always up to the challenge. On the other hand, some people claim that there are no inherent rights or wrongs that we should respect but only values that we choose for ourselves, yet they often speak as though others really *ought* to share their values of fairness or honesty. Such inconsistency is a common mark of our human frailty—our failure to "get our act together." It does not follow that we do not *have* a worldview but only that we fail to live by one consistently.

> It is difficult to imagine that anyone could live without at least the rudiments of a worldview: without *some* sense that certain activities are more worthwhile than others, that certain goals are worth pursuing and others are not, that some of our impulses may rightly be indulged while others should not, and so on.

5. Many people are unable to articulate a worldview of their own: either they have not thought seriously about the matter or they have been unable to make up their minds on fundamental questions. Does this mean that they do not *have* a worldview?

Our answer to this question will depend on the degree to which we demand clarity and coherence of thought before we credit people with having a worldview. It is difficult to imagine that anyone could live without at least the rudiments of a worldview: without *some* sense that certain activities are more worthwhile than others, that certain goals are worth pursuing and others are not, that some of our impulses may rightly be indulged while others should not, and so on. We may not ourselves have sorted out the implications, but when we regard certain actions (but not others) as "worthwhile" or "right," we imply that there is something about ourselves or our world that makes things worthwhile or right. At least at an implicit level, then, worldviews do seem an integral part of human living. (There is, however, something to be said for being able to say *why* we do what we do and make the choices we make.)

6. On the other hand, a number of people today would claim that all worldviews are mere human constructions, artificial patterns that we concoct in our minds and that correspond to nothing in reality. We cannot pause here to examine such a claim. We may simply note that in order to deny that any worldview corresponds to reality, one must have a certain understanding of reality—in other words, a worldview. It follows that the worldview that says that all worldviews are false cannot be right without being wrong.[8]

> Understanding another person's worldview may mean coming to see, in terms compatible with one's *own* worldview, how others could think quite differently.

7. Although no one can hold more than one worldview simultaneously, befriending, or even peacefully coexisting with, other people frequently requires that we make some attempt to understand where they are coming from. But what would it mean to "understand" another person's worldview? Broadly speaking, two possibilities suggest themselves.[9]

a. In the example given above, Barney understands Bernie as one who has projected his wishes onto the universe, and Bernie

---

8. Put differently, the claim that all worldviews are mere human constructions corresponding to nothing in reality really means that all worldviews are false except this one. In that respect it differs from other worldviews on the market only by being obviously self-contradictory.

9. In important respects the two possibilities for understanding another's worldview are analogous to the two ways of reading texts discussed in the introduction above. The first approach, in each case, is taken by one who is not attentive to the words or thinking of another *as* other but only as it can be categorized within one's present ways of thinking. The second approach takes an interest precisely in others' *otherness*.

understands Barney as one who has lost or suppressed his sense of the wonder and goodness of life. In both these cases, understanding means coming to see, in terms compatible with one's own worldview, how others could think quite differently. Barney believes there is no God, but he can hardly be unaware of the Bernies in the world who think there is. He may, of course, simply ignore the questions raised by their faith. But if he confronts them seriously, he must either adopt for himself the faith of Bernie or explain to himself how people such as Bernie have come to hold what he takes to be the false belief that there is a God. Barney chooses the latter alternative. The result is an explanation of religious faith that suits the *non*religious framework within which Barney lives: an explanation of the way Bernie thinks that Bernie himself would not recognize, although it satisfies Barney. (In secular schools of learning, such explanations of religion are legion.) Conversely, Bernie believes there is a God, but he can hardly be unaware of the Barneys in the world who think there is not. He may simply ignore the questions raised by their lack of faith. But if he confronts them seriously, he must either abandon his own faith or explain—to his own satisfaction, at least—why people such as Barney believe there is no God, even though Bernie is sure that there is. Bernie chooses the latter alternative. The result is an explanation of unbelief that suits the religious framework within which Bernie lives: an explanation of the way Barney thinks that Barney himself would not recognize, although it satisfies Bernie. (In religious circles, such explanations of unbelief are legion.)

There is some substance to the charge that both Barney and Bernie are guilty of a kind of cultural imperialism: neither allows any real significance to the way the other sees things, both squeeze the other into the mould of their own thinking, both believe at heart that they understand the other better than the other understands himself. Cultural imperialism has a bad press; yet in the end, in my view, neither Barney nor Bernie should be faulted for attempting to find a place within their own intellectual horizons for the positions of others. Indeed, the alternatives—either ignoring the otherness of others or abandoning one's own position whenever one encounters people who think differently—seem much less desirable. There is, moreover, in any serious attempt to come to grips with the views of others the possibility that we will come to a better understanding of the world we live in. Still, finding a way to explain the thinking of others from within one's own horizons is hardly the only way to understand them—nor does it lead to the type of understanding that promotes friendship (or even peaceful coexistence).

　　b. The second way of understanding others is to strive to see, to the extent that it is possible, how things look to *them*; to learn how one would account for the phenomena of life in *their* terms, whether or not these terms have a place within our own worldview. Of course we can never (to repeat the hackneyed expression) really step inside another person's shoes. But our understanding of others is rather limited if we fail to see how things make sense to them or how a sane person could think the way they do. Coming to see how a sane person could think differently than we do by no means implies that we abandon our own way of thinking (although we might find reasons for doing so). But understanding others in this way is much more likely to promote peaceful coexistence, genuine sympathy, and even friendship than the kind of understanding that reduces the thinking and practices of others to categories suited to our own ways of thinking.

> The second way of understanding others is to strive to see, to the extent that it is possible, how things look to *them*; to learn how one would account for the phenomena of life in *their* terms, whether or not these terms have a place within our own worldview.

　　Once the important distinction between these two types of understanding is recognized, there is, I believe, a place for both. But it is the second type of understanding that will be pursued here. Exposed to different aspects of Matthew's way of thinking, readers will no doubt vary considerably in the extent to which they find them compatible with their own. Still, the goal of a book such as this is that every reader will begin to understand how Matthew made sense of things, and to see how it makes sense to make sense of things that way.

2

No Worry, No Fear

$\mathbb{A}$mong the best-known and most controversial words of Jesus in Matthew's Gospel are the following:

No one can serve two masters; for a slave will either hate the one and love the other, or be devoted to the one and despise the other. You cannot serve God and wealth.[1]

Therefore I tell you, do not worry about your life, what you will eat or what you will drink, or about your body, what you will wear. Is not life more than food, and the body more than clothing? Look at the birds of the air; they neither sow nor reap nor gather into barns, and yet your heavenly Father feeds them. Are you not of more value than they? And can any of you by worrying add a single hour to your span of life? And why do you worry about clothing? Consider the lilies of the field, how they grow; they neither toil nor spin, yet I tell you, even Solomon in all his glory was not clothed like one of these. But if God so clothes the grass of the field, which is alive today and tomorrow is thrown into the oven, will he not much more clothe you—you of little faith? Therefore do not worry, saying, "What will we eat?" or "What will we drink?" or "What will we wear?" For it is the Gentiles who strive for all these things; and indeed your heavenly Father knows that you need all these things. But strive first for the

---

1. These last words as they appear in the King James Version have become proverbial in English: "Ye cannot serve God and mammon."

kingdom of God and his righteousness, and all these things will be
given to you as well.[2]

So do not worry about tomorrow, for tomorrow will bring worries
of its own. Today's trouble is enough for today.[3]

Words from a Different World

We can hardly read these verses without sensing at once that
they come from a world very different from our own. Jesus
simply assumes that the people to whom he speaks believe
that there is a God and that God is their benevolent heavenly
Father.[4]

To people who share with him these common convictions,
Jesus points out that their behavior should reflect their beliefs.
As we noted in chapter 1, our immediate needs and desires
tend to dominate our thinking; as a result, even people who
believe in an afterlife often fail to consider, before they choose,
what action would best promote their well-being in the *long*
run. Jesus' words point to a similar inconsistency. It is human
to worry. But children of the well-to-do do not worry where
their next meal is coming from; neither should people who
believe that a benevolent God is their heavenly Father. If God
has given us life and our bodies, he will surely not leave us
without food, clothing, and shelter. He cares for the birds. He
gives flowers their beauty. He can be counted on to meet the
needs of humans as well. Besides, worry serves no purpose: no
amount of worry will add years (or even hours) to our lives.
So we can leave worrying to people who do not know God
and think they must fend for themselves. Those who truly
know God will trust him and want to live for him.[5] They can
no more share their devotion for God with a pursuit of wealth

2. That is, "God will give you all these things [life's necessities] as well as a place
in his kingdom."

3. Matthew 6:24–34.

4. Jesus is speaking to his disciples. But Jews who did not follow Jesus still shared
a belief in God's existence and goodness.

5. For the moment, "Live for God" will serve as a rough equivalent to "Strive first
for the kingdom of God and his righteousness" (Matthew 6:33). In subsequent chapters we will look at what Matthew means by the "kingdom of God" (or "kingdom of
heaven") and how he thinks its citizens are to live.

than a slave can be at the beck and call of different masters. But since God is their master, they can count on him to give them all they need.

Such, in brief, is Jesus' argument—and as noted above, it comes from a different world. It is easy to see why people who believe in a benevolent God might need Jesus' reminder not to worry. Yet even they might be left uneasy by parts of Jesus' argument. That worrying does not add to the length of our lives is a fair observation. But if well-fed birds are a sign of a benevolent providence, what, we might wonder, are starving birds a sign of? Or starving people, for that matter? Even believers, we might think, must see that real life is not as simple as Jesus portrays it. For people who see no reason to believe in God, however, the passage is problematic from start to finish. In the example in the previous chapter, Barney represented people of that persuasion. We will let him do so here again.

> It is easy to see why people who believe in a benevolent God might need Jesus' reminder not to worry. Yet even they might be left uneasy by parts of Jesus' argument.

Somewhat surprisingly, perhaps, Barney first reads Jesus' words with considerable sympathy. He has seen a good deal of the corporate rat race; at times he feels as though he would like nothing better than to be done with it. A friend once told him that people on their deathbed never wish they had spent more time at the office, and Barney sees the point. There is more to life, he has come to think, than getting ahead in business. And there is more to life, too, he realizes, than surrounding himself with all the things that getting ahead in business allows him to buy—acquiring, for example, the most luxurious car with the most labor-saving buttons so that he can drive in maximum style, comfort, and ease to his favorite fitness club for a strenuous workout. Or equipping his living room with an entertainment center so sophisticated that he can recline in his easy chair and imagine himself out in the forest among the trees, the birds, and the butterflies. Could he not, it has occurred to him, achieve nearly the same effect by going for a walk—and at the same time save himself the expense of membership in a fitness club?

So Barney has come to think; and on first reading Matthew, he imagines that Jesus is a kindred spirit. What, after all, is the point of accumulating stuff on earth? "Whoever dies with the most toys wins"? Why get enslaved by the chase for wealth? Who needs ulcers anyway? Why not get back to a simpler lifestyle, to appreciating nature—the birds and the flowers? Is that not what Jesus is saying?

A second reading, however, convinces Barney that it is not. Jesus wants his hearers to turn from a life of wealth and worry, it is true; but the alternative he proposes is a life devoted to the service of God. Barney does not believe in God, for starters; and any God he ever *could* believe in would let Barney get on with his life without demanding any "service." As for believing that God will provide his necessities, Barney thinks that this would be like assuming you have money in the bank to pay your bills when in fact your funds are exhausted: it would be a big mistake to count on God to show up when you need him. Nor is Barney convinced that nature is brimming with proofs of divine providence; nature, for him, means the survival of the fittest. Barney still sees no reason for believing in God; but after reading Jesus' words, he is more convinced than ever that his explanation of others' belief is on target. Are not Jesus' words the perfect example of projecting on to the universe a naive desire for the security of a warm home overseen by a benevolent "heavenly Father"?

> Are not Jesus' words an example of projecting on to the universe a naive desire for the security of a warm home overseen by a benevolent "heavenly Father"?

Yet however remote Jesus' way of thinking may seem to Barney, it made sense to people at the time of Jesus and has continued to make sense to many people since. We can, of course, dismiss them all as fools and dreamers; many do. But we have made it our goal to try to see things the way Jesus (and Matthew) sees them. Since a narrative is better than an argument for helping us see things differently, we will first allow Barney's friend Bernie to represent those to whom Jesus' words make sense. Then we will look briefly at other passages in Matthew that build on the same convictions we find in Matthew 6. We will conclude this chapter by seeing how these convictions shaped Dietrich Bonhoeffer's view of life in a Nazi prison.

The Worldview of Christians (*and* Jews *and* Muslims)

First, Bernie. Bernie would say that he has always believed in God, but he would also admit that this belief did not really penetrate much of his thinking before his baby was born. He was always a decent enough person. And for years he pursued his goal to become the best biologist he could possibly be with real dedication and discipline. But Bernie's whole outlook on life changed with the birth of his baby. (This is not unusual.) Two aspects of the change are of interest to us here.

First, Bernie now sees himself as having obligations to meet—and frankly, he has never seriously thought this way before. He has always been very focused, very disciplined. But he disciplined himself not because he thought he ought to do so but simply because he had goals he wanted to achieve. Now, suddenly, he has had an insight, an intuition, an "aha!" experience (or whatever you want to call it), and it has left him with the fundamental conviction, the sense in his bones, that he has obligations to fulfill toward another human being. The way he now sees things, his baby needs to be cared for; and since he had a part in bringing the child into the world, he has a duty to see to it that the baby's needs are met.

> After the birth of his daughter, Bernie senses that he has obligations to fulfill toward another human being and that it would be wrong to neglect them.

Decent chap that he is, Bernie takes his responsibility seriously. He finds himself getting up at all hours of the night, much against his wishes. It would be nice if we could think that he gets up because he loves his baby; if the truth be told, however, love is not uppermost in Bernie's thinking when he is awakened by his screaming offspring. He gets up anyway, though, because he senses that he should. It would be wrong, he feels, to neglect his baby's needs.

Barney's wife, too, has recently had a baby, and Barney knows something of what Bernie is feeling. What is more, Barney believes that he can explain Bernie's sense of obligation. It comes from one of two sources (Barney is not inclined to decide between them): genes or environment. Either, in the course of evolution, human beings have developed instincts that promote the preservation of the species, and such an instinct is the source of Bernie's feeling that he ought to care for his baby, or Bernie has been brought up and educated to think it his duty to do so.

Bernie, hearing Barney's explanations, is not impressed. Evolution may explain Bernie's instinct to care for his child; it cannot turn that instinct into an obligation. Other instincts (like the instinct to punch in the nose a person with whom one disagrees) are scarcely obligations. If anything, we have an obligation to stifle some of our instincts. Why ought Bernie to follow one instinct and not another? Why is he *obligated* to care for his child?

> Our obligations are real, Bernie is convinced, and they are not the same as our instincts; nor do they always correspond with what we have been brought up to think.

The same problem arises with the suggestion that Bernie has been brought up to think that he ought to care for his child. Bernie was also brought up to enjoy baseball. But caring for babies is an obligation and enjoying baseball is not. For that matter, Bernie might well have been brought up (as many people are) to think that he ought to hate people of a different race or religion; but if he was, Bernie is now convinced that it would be wrong to do so. Real obligations and what we have been brought up to think we ought to do are not necessarily the same thing.

In short, Bernie thinks Barney is missing the boat. Barney can try to explain why Bernie, in his better moments, at least, *feels* that he ought to care for his child. Barney cannot explain why, whether Bernie feels like it or not, he *has* an obligation to care for his child—and Bernie is convinced that he does. Barney's inability to explain Bernie's obligation suggests to Bernie a blind spot in Barney's way of looking at things.

This, of course, Barney is not prepared to concede. When he hears that Bernie is not satisfied with his explanations, he suggests that Bernie's talk of an obligation is itself misguided. It is not that he *ought* to care for his baby. Caring for babies is simply one of the values Bernie has chosen to live by. Some people value some things, other people others. Bernie values caring for his baby. Good for him! But we must not jump from a choice that Bernie happens to have made to an obligation binding on anyone and everyone who has a part in bringing a child into the world.

Bernie hears this explanation and rolls his eyes in disbelief. If caring for children were only a matter of one's preferred values or choices, he might well choose to do it *some*times, but definitely not at others! Yet he knows in his heart that, regardless of his preferences or choices, it would be wrong for him to neglect that ten-pound bundle of screams and tears that completely depends on her parents.

And do not tell Bernie that he is supposed to care for his daughter because the law says that he should. As if parents' duties to their children started when politicians got around to taking a vote! As if he would not have a duty to care for his kid if he lived in Jokolomono, where there is no such law! The suggestion, Bernie is convinced, is preposterous. Laws may enforce parents' duties to their children; they cannot be the source of those duties.

Aha! thinks Barney. Mention Jokolomono and he can *prove* that Bernie is wrong. Does he not know that in societies like Jokolomono parents do not always care for their offspring? Some societies (like Jokolomono, for all Barney knows) kill twins when they are born. Others abandon baby girls just because they are girls, or expose whatever infants are unwanted. How can Bernie speak of an obligation to care for children when not all parents feel this way? Bernie just happens to have been brought up differently.

Bernie is not biting. He is well aware that different societies think differently in any number of ways. But he is not convinced that the different ways they think are equally right. After all, whole societies have had crazy ideas about geography, medicine, astrology, and alchemy, but no one thinks this an argument for getting rid of our textbooks about geography, medicine, astronomy, and chemistry. It simply means that whole societies can be wrong. Can we not just say—*must* we not just say?—that whole societies are wrong if they kill baby twins or abandon baby girls or expose unwanted infants?

For the moment we need not pursue Barney and Bernie's debate any further; we need only say that Bernie's way of looking at things represents one aspect of the way religious Jews and Christians and Muslims (and many others) think. They all believe that, of course, Bernie should care for his child. Their only question would be how he has lived so many years without realizing that he has had obligations all along. Has he never made a promise? Does he not realize that he ought to keep his promises, that it would be wrong if he failed to do so? Has he never been given anything? Does he not realize that he ought to say thank you, that it would be wrong to take from others without responding with gratitude? Has he never written a letter, or paid a visit, or helped somebody across the street, *not* because he felt like doing it, but because it was the right thing to do? In all of life—Jews, Christians, and Muslims believe—we face choices between right and wrong, good and evil; and which we choose says something about the kind of people we are.

But back to Bernie—and to the second aspect of his life that was changed by his baby's birth. It is scary to think that a tiny human life completely depends on you to survive and grow; but this is hardly the whole story. Bernie is thrilled too—thrilled as he has never been thrilled before. He has a *child*! He and his wife have a *baby*! Incredible!

> In all of life—Jews, Christians, Muslims, and many others believe—we face choices between right and wrong, good and evil; and which we choose says something about the kind of people we are.

Indeed, it is more than incredible; it is a *miracle*.

So Bernie feels. And there is nothing particularly remarkable about his feelings; many parents feel the same way. Our Bernie, though, is different. He cannot help wondering what this awesome event really means.

The only way he can begin to describe what has happened is to say that he has been given a gift, a wonderful gift. Not that he *owns* his baby, of course. From day one, she is her own unique person, and Bernie knows this. But he still feels that he has been entrusted with a baby, so to speak. And though being entrusted with a child is certainly scary, it is awesome too. An awesome gift.

Why a *gift*? For one thing, because the girl with whom he has been entrusted is precious beyond description. He knows that he would not give up his daughter for any amount of money. When we talk about the value of money and the value of a baby's life, we talk about things so different, so incomparable, that we really should not use the same word, "value," to describe both. Bernie's baby's life is precious beyond money, beyond description.

And she is a *gift* because he knows he has not done anything to deserve her. Of course, he had a role in his baby's conception. Actually, he and Bertha had *not* planned to have a baby just now; but even if they had, as we put it, "planned" to have her, the conception and development and birth of their baby were, in so many ways, so completely out of their control that we cannot really talk about her life as the product of their planning at all.

And yet it happened. The baby was conceived, and she grew and developed nerves and muscles and a heart that beats and lungs that breathe and a brain that functions—all the amazing things that happen in the womb without our doing anything about them. And the result is the wonderful gift of a child that you never earn but that you are entrusted with nonetheless. Bernie feels that he has been blessed with a child, and he is grateful.

> Something more is going on than the mechanics of conception and cellular growth when a *person* is born.

Barney, however, cannot see the point. Grateful? Why grateful? Sperm meets egg cell; sperm fertilizes egg cell; fertilized cell moves to uterus; cell cluster develops into embryo; embryo develops organs and limbs—and so on until the baby is born. What is the big deal?

Bernie shakes his head. He knows all that stuff. And of course, on one level, it is all true. But it is hardly the whole story. Analyzing the birth of a child on this level strikes Bernie as like reading the Gettysburg Address only to analyze its sentence structure, or listening to a Beethoven symphony only to analyze its harmonic progressions. Of *course* Lincoln's speech is made up of a combination of simple, compound, and complex sentences; but it *means* something too. Of *course* the harmonic progressions in a symphony can be analyzed; but that is not all that hearing a symphony is about. Bernie feels the same way about his daughter's birth. He is familiar with the "facts of life" and does not dispute any of them. But he still insists that something more is going on than the mechanics of conception and cellular growth when a human being is born—a *person*, his baby daughter. It is awesome. He can only describe it as a gift.

Whether we ourselves think along the same lines as Barney or Bernie or neither in particular, we will never begin to understand Matthew (or Christians in general, or religious Jews or

Muslims) if we cannot at least relate to Bernie's way of thinking. Jews, Christians, and Muslims feel about all of life the way Bernie feels about his daughter. They agree with Bernie that he has been entrusted with a gift. They only wonder how he came this far without realizing that he has been showered with incredible gifts every day of his life: it is about time he started feeling a bit grateful! Every day that dawns is a new gift. Every breath he breathes, every beat of his heart, every impulse of his brain is incredibly wonderful and yet, in many ways, out of his power to control. It is a gift that he is able to run and shoot hoops and appreciate music and know love and laughter and a good meal. Granted, on one level there are matter-of-fact explanations of how all these things work. But they only explain on one level. When we laugh or fall in love, there is more going on than random impulses in our brain and movements of our nerves and muscles—just as there is more to the Gettysburg Address than a combination of different sentence structures, and more to a Beethoven symphony than harmonic progressions. There is a *goodness* in all these things, and we ought to be grateful.

A Jewish thinker put it this way:

> There is no worship, no music, no love, if we take for granted the blessings or defeats of living. No routine of the social, physical, or physiological order must dull our sense of surprise at the fact that there *is* a social, a physical, or a physiological order. We [Jews] are trained in maintaining our sense of wonder by uttering a prayer before the enjoyment of food. Each time we are about to drink a glass of water, we remind ourselves of the eternal mystery of creation, "Blessed be Thou . . . by whose word all things come into being."

> There is thus only one way to wisdom: awe. Forfeit your sense of awe, let your conceit diminish your ability to revere, and the universe becomes a market place for you. The loss of awe is the great block to insight. A return to reverence is the first prerequisite for a revival of wisdom, for the discovery of the world as an allusion to God.[6]

The same point is made frequently in the Koran.

6. Abraham Joshua Heschel, *God in Search of Man: A Philosophy of Judaism* (New York: Farrar, Straus & Giroux, 1955), 49, 78.

Why . . . do you not reflect? Consider the seeds you grow. Is it you that give them growth, or We [= God]? . . . Consider the water which you drink. Was it you that poured it from the cloud, or We? If We pleased, We could turn it bitter. Why, then, do you not give thanks? Observe the fire which you light. Is it you that create its wood, or We? We have made it a reminder for man, and for the traveller, a comfort. Praise, then, the name of your Lord, the Supreme One.[7]

Barney's outlook on life, Bernie feels, leaves him with no explanation of a parent's *obligation* (or of right and wrong in general) and no sensitivity to the wonder and goodness of life. Bernie himself, sensing both, can relate at once to Jesus' words about the heavenly Father in whose benevolence we may trust.

Other Evidence in Matthew

Along lines like these perhaps even disenchanted readers in the twenty-first century may begin to see how for Matthew, Jesus, and millions of others, the world is charged with the glory and goodness of God. Where this sense is missing, the teaching and demands of Jesus seem to lack footing in the real world. Where it is present, much becomes immediately intelligible. For Jesus, God's goodness was palpably real, and it governed his whole way of thinking. "Don't worry about trivialities like food and clothing—leave them to your Father in heaven to provide!" is a fine example. But there are many others.

> For Matthew, Jesus, and millions of others, the world is charged with the glory and goodness of God. Where this sense is missing, the teaching and demands of Jesus seem to lack footing in the real world. Where it is present, much becomes immediately intelligible.

Ask, and it will be given you; search, and you will find; knock, and the door will be opened for you. For everyone who asks receives, and everyone who searches finds, and for everyone who knocks, the door will be opened. Is there anyone among you who, if your child asks for bread, will give a stone? Or if the child asks for

7. 56:62–74. From *The Koran*, trans. N. J. Dawood (Harmondsworth: Penguin, 1995), 380.

a fish, will give a snake? If you then, who are evil, know how to give good gifts to your children, how much more will your Father in heaven give good things to those who ask him![8]

The point of these verses is missed if we think Jesus is offering his disciples a glorified Alladin's lamp to grant all their wishes. No wise father indulges his children's most capricious wishes—and the God of Jesus is nothing if not a wise Father. Not the magical properties of a lamp but the limitless goodwill of the Father in heaven is the point of Jesus' words. To God we may come confidently for everything we need. He is the prototypical Father of whom the best earthly father is but a poor imitation.

The need for trust (or "faith") in God is stated repeatedly throughout Matthew's Gospel.[9] It is Jesus' most basic requirement. God's benevolence is assured; if people fail to experience God's favor, it is only because they fail to trust him sufficiently to bring their needs to him:[10] "According to your faith let it be done to you."[11] So real is Jesus' own sense of God's goodness that he can only shake his head at the "little faith" of his disciples.[12]

One cannot sense the limitless goodness of God, however, without *loving* God as well—nor can one love God unless one senses and trusts God's goodness. Loving God, then, with "all" one's "heart," "soul," and "mind" (with all one's being, in other words), is "the greatest and first commandment."[13] The Barneys of the world may have no sympathy for any god who does not leave them alone to live their own lives. The Bernies of the world, on the other hand, sense that divine love underlies our world and sustains our existence; and they know that they would be false to what is most real and true and good in all of life if they were

8. Matthew 7:7–11.

9. Note also how the instructions Jesus gives to his disciples in Matthew 10:9–10 leave them dependent on God for both food (they are to carry neither money nor provisions) and protection (they are to travel without the staff that they would otherwise use to defend themselves against human or animal attack).

10. Repeatedly in Matthew's Gospel, God's goodwill toward people and God's power to help them in their need are reflected in Jesus' own activity, and it is in Jesus that people put their trust (see, for example, Matthew 8:2–3, 5–13, 16; 9:2–8, 18–26, 27–31). We will be examining Jesus' relationship with God in chapter 6, below.

11. Matthew 9:29; see also 8:13.

12. See Matthew 6:30; 8:26; 14:31; 16:8; 17:20.

13. Matthew 22:37–38.

to do anything other than live in its light and devote themselves to its service. Just as the focus and delight of people in love centers on their beloved, and joy in their beloved transforms all their other occupations and relationships, so devotion to God is necessarily an all-consuming passion. It is the pure in heart who will see God.[14] To know, trust, and love God, Jesus says, is like having one's vision suffused with light. To live without God, by way of contrast, is to walk in the dark.[15]

> Divine love underlies our world and sustains our existence. We are false to what is most real and true and good in all of life if we fail to live in its light or devote ourselves to its service.

What about Birds That Starve?

Real life, we may well think, is not so simple. In the real world, birds die of starvation. And people get killed—even people who trust in God. We would, of course, be foolish to think that the unsavory aspects of life are a modern discovery. Our passage in Matthew 6 reminds us that every day has its troubles.[16] Elsewhere in the Gospel Jesus tells those who would follow him to expect deprivation, on the one hand, and opposition, on the other:

A scribe then approached and said, "Teacher, I will follow you wherever you go." And Jesus said to him, "Foxes have holes, and birds of the air have nests; but the Son of Man has nowhere to lay his head."[17]

Do not fear those who kill the body but cannot kill the soul; rather fear [God] who can destroy both soul and body in hell. Are not two sparrows sold for a penny? Yet not one of them will fall to the ground apart

14. Matthew 5:8.
15. This seems to be the point of Matthew 6:22–23: "The eye is the lamp of the body. So, if your eye is healthy [if, that is, you live singlemindedly for God and his goodness], your whole body will be full of light; but if your eye is unhealthy [if, that is, you live without God or divide your devotion between God and wealth], your whole body will be full of darkness. If then the light in you is darkness, how great is the darkness!"
16. Matthew 6:34.
17. Matthew 8:19–20.

from your Father. And even the hairs of your head are all counted. So
do not be afraid; you are of more value than many sparrows.[18]

These verses introduce several themes to be considered in
subsequent chapters. For the moment, three observations must
suffice.

1. The worldview reflected in these verses clearly takes into
account that sparrows fall to the ground and die and that people
who trust in God may be left without shelter—or may even be
put to death. (We may add, of course, that in the Gospel of Matthew Jesus is crucified.) At least in these verses, however, no
explanation is given *why* bad things happen to birds and good
people. We will return to the subject below.

2. Those who sense the wonder and goodness of life and
of the God who gives it must conclude, when bad things happen, either that their sense of life's underlying goodness was
mistaken or that, ultimately, life remains good and bad things
have an explanation. Matthew's Gospel takes bad things into
account but remains convinced of the providence and benevolence of God. The same can, of course, be said of the Bible as
a whole.

> As for me, I am poor and needy,
>   but the Lord takes thought for me.[19]

> My flesh and my heart may fail,
>   but God is the strength of my
>   heart and my portion forever.[20]

3. In the second quotation above, Jesus tells his disciples
to fear God—and God alone. Those who fear God, in other
words, need fear no one (and nothing) else.[21] The logic is the
same as that in Matthew 6: a right relationship with the King
of the universe relieves those who trust him of the anxieties
and fears that trouble others who imagine they must fend for
themselves.

18. Matthew 10:28–31.
19. Psalm 40:17.
20. Psalm 73:26.
21. The same point is made in Isaiah 8:11–13.

God's Goodness and Nazi Prisons

> A right relationship with the King of the universe relieves those who trust him of the anxieties and fears that trouble others who imagine they must fend for themselves.

Dietrich Bonhoeffer was arrested by the Gestapo on April 5, 1943. The rest of his life was spent in Nazi prisons.[22] Much of his correspondence that survived the war—both letters that he was allowed to write and others that were smuggled out of prison—was collected and published in what has become his best-known book, *Letters and Papers from Prison*.[23]

This collection has more recently been supplemented by what survives of his correspondence with his fiancée, Maria von Wedemeyer.[24] Their relationship began in earnest in the summer of 1942.[25] Bonhoeffer had just returned from Sweden, where he had informed Dr. George Bell, bishop of Chichester, of plans for a coup d'état in Germany; the information was to be passed on to the British government. Bonhoeffer, who knew himself already to be under Gestapo surveillance, met Maria at her grandmother's house. The relationship blossomed quickly. In November, however, Maria's mother requested that the two break off contact with each other for a year; she sensed that Dietrich was in danger, and thought Maria too young for an engagement in any case. They did not see each other again before Dietrich's arrest, although on January 13, 1943, Maria wrote to Dietrich of her willingness to marry him. After Dietrich's imprisonment, his meetings with Maria were few: they spent a total of eight hours together in the first year of their engagement, always in the presence of prison guards. The letters they exchanged add an important dimension to our understanding of Bonhoeffer's thoughts during this period.

Throughout the correspondence and in a variety of contexts, Bonhoeffer expressed his confidence in God's goodness and care.

22. He was executed on April 9, 1945.

23. Dietrich Bonhoeffer, *Letters and Papers from Prison*, ed. Eberhard Bethge, expanded ed. (New York: Simon & Schuster, 1997).

24. Dietrich Bonhoeffer, *Love Letters from Cell 92*, ed. Ruth-Alice von Bismarck and Ulrich Kabitz (London: HarperCollins, 1995).

25. The two had met earlier, when Maria was a child.

[*To Maria*] It's very reassuring to know you're busy with your trousseau. I picture that in every detail and in full colour, and I'm glad of it; it's such an image of calm, confidence, and happiness. When shall I see and admire and delight in all those things? And when shall we use them together in our daily life and, at the same time, recall the strange times in which they originated? It can't be very much longer. But we'll be patient to the last and look upon this difficult time of waiting, too, as God's way with us, until one day, perhaps, we gain a better understanding of why it was good for us.[26]

[*To Maria*] God is forever upsetting our plans, but only in order to fulfil his own, better plans through us.[27]

[*To Renate and Eberhard Bethge, Dietrich's niece and his best friend, before the baptism of their first child*] I shouldn't like the thought of my absence to cast the least shadow on your happiness. . . . I believe that nothing that happens to me is meaningless, and that it is good for us all that it should be so, even if it runs counter to our own wishes. As I see it, I'm here for some purpose, and I only hope I may fulfil it. In the light of the great purpose all our privations and disappointments are trivial. Nothing would be more unworthy and wrongheaded than to turn one of those rare occasions of joy, such as you're now experiencing, into a calamity because of my present situation.[28]

[*To Eberhard Bethge*] Please don't ever get anxious or worried about me, but don't forget to pray for me—I'm sure you don't! I am so sure of God's guiding hand that I hope I shall always be kept in that certainty. You must never doubt that I'm travelling with gratitude and cheerfulness along the road where I'm being led. My past life is brim-full of God's goodness, and my sins are covered by the forgiving love of Christ crucified. I'm most thankful for the people I have met, and I only hope that they never have to grieve about me, but that they, too, will always be certain of, and thankful for, God's mercy and forgiveness.[29]

> "You must never doubt that I'm travelling with gratitude and cheerfulness along the road where I'm being led."

26. Bonhoeffer, *Love Letters*, 64.
27. Ibid., 186.
28. Bonhoeffer, *Letters and Papers*, 289–90.
29. Ibid., 393.

Bonhoeffer's assurance that God was directing his paths freed him from second thoughts and regrets about actions that precipitated his arrest.

[*To Eberhard Bethge*] I'm often surprised how little (in contrast to nearly all the others here) I grub among my past mistakes and think how different one thing or another would be today if I had acted differently in the past; it doesn't worry me at all. Everything seems to have taken its natural course, and to be determined necessarily and straightforwardly by a higher providence. Do you feel the same?[30]

[*To Hans von Dohnanyi, Dietrich's brother-in-law*] You must know that there is not even an atom of reproach or bitterness in me about what has befallen the two of us. Such things come from God and from him alone. . . . Until recently . . . we have been able to enjoy so many good things together that it would be almost presumptuous were we not also ready to accept hardship quietly, bravely—and also really gratefully.[31]

Yet Bonhoeffer was no Stoic: whatever inner peace he may have experienced, it was not purchased at the price of indifference toward the world around him. Life's *goodness* required celebrating—even in a Nazi prison.

[*To Maria*] It's odd: in a cell you learn to think in lengthy periods of time, but when something you've definitely been counting on, a letter or a parcel, turns up even a little bit late, you become fidgety and get silly ideas, and you keep telling yourself that's all they are, silly ideas. That's how it is unless you're a Stoic, which I'm not and have no wish to be.[32]

[*To his parents*] Here in the prison yard there is a thrush which sings beautifully in the morning, and now in the evening too. One is grateful for little things, and that is surely a gain.[33]

[*To Renate and Eberhard Bethge*] I think we honour God more if we gratefully accept the life that he gives us with all its blessings, loving it and drinking it to the full, and also grieving deeply and sincerely when we have impaired or wasted any of the good things of life . . . ,

30. Ibid., 276.
31. Ibid., 31–32.
32. Bonhoeffer, *Love Letters*, 64.
33. Bonhoeffer, *Letters and Papers*, 22.

than if we are insensitive to life's blessings and may therefore also be insensitive to pain.[34]

For Bonhoeffer, faith in God's goodness meant relishing all that life—here and now, in *this* world—has to offer. He had no use for the suggestion from Maria's (very spiritually minded!) mother that he and Maria should devote their prison visits to something "important"—like reading the Bible and praying.

Well, Maria, the whole idea is impossible, and I would find it alien and unnatural. We shouldn't "make" something of our brief moments together—no, that's out. . . . I simply want you as you are in reality, without effort or deliberation. That's "greater" and far more "important" than any "importance" and "greatness," because it's real life, just as it flows from the hand of God.[35]

[*To Eberhard Bethge*] It is only when one loves life and the earth so much that without them everything seems to be over that one may believe in the resurrection and a new world.[36]

[*To Eberhard Bethge*] To put it plainly, for a man in his wife's arms to be hankering after the other world is, in mild terms, a piece of bad taste, and not God's will. We ought to find and love God in what he actually gives us.[37]

[*To Eberhard Bethge*] God wants us to love him eternally with our whole hearts—not in such a way as to injure or weaken our earthly love, but to provide a kind of *cantus firmus*[38] to which the other melodies of life provide the counterpoint. One of these contrapuntal themes (which have their own complete independence but are yet related to the *cantus firmus*) is earthly affection.[39]

Bonhoeffer saw an important parallel between an incident in the life of the Old Testament prophet Jeremiah and his own

34. Ibid., 191–92.
35. Bonhoeffer, *Love Letters*, 168.
36. Bonhoeffer, *Letters and Papers*, 157.
37. Ibid., 168.
38. That is, a musical tune to which other voices are added. Counterpoint (or contrapuntal music) is music in which different voices, each interesting in itself, are combined to produce a more intricate beauty.
39. Bonhoeffer, *Letters and Papers*, 303.

situation. When Jerusalem was under siege and about to fall to the Babylonians, God told the prophet to purchase a field.[40] Jeremiah, questioning the business acumen of the Almighty, pointed out that this was no time to be investing in real estate. He was told that the purchase was a sign that, present circumstances notwithstanding, God would one day restore his people's fortunes; "houses and fields and vineyards [would] again be bought in this land."[41] Bonhoeffer cited the incident in a letter to Maria;[42] their relationship, in circumstances that were anything but promising, was similarly

> "For a man in his wife's arms to be hankering after the other world is, in mild terms, a piece of bad taste, and not God's will. We ought to find and love God in what he actually gives us."

> a token of confidence in the future. That requires faith, and may God grant us it daily. . . . Our marriage must be a "yes" to God's earth. It must strengthen our resolve to do and accomplish something on earth. I fear that Christians who venture to stand on earth on only one leg will stand in heaven on only one leg too.[43]

Dark hours, Dietrich wrote to Maria shortly before Christmas 1943, lamenting their separation, were inevitable. So, too, were questions of "Why?"

> How hard it is, inwardly to accept what defies our understanding; how great is the temptation to feel ourselves at the mercy of blind chance; . . . and how readily we fall prey to the childish notion that the course of our lives reposes in human hands! And then, just when everything is bearing down on us to such an extent that we can scarcely withstand it, the Christmas message comes to tell us that all our ideas are wrong, and that what we take to be evil and dark is really good and light because it comes from God. Our eyes are at fault, that is all. God is in the manger, wealth in poverty, light in darkness, succour in abandonment. No evil can befall us; whatever men may do to us, they cannot but serve the God who is secretly revealed as love and rules the world and our lives.[44]

---

40. See the discussion in chapter 4, below, under the heading "The Babylonian Exile."
41. Jeremiah 32:15.
42. See also Bonhoeffer, *Letters and Papers*, 15.
43. Bonhoeffer, *Love Letters*, 48–49.
44. Ibid., 109.

3

Who *Does* That?

The Gospel of Matthew is full of demands that most everybody knows and most nobody follows: "Don't worry!" in Matthew 6 (which we have just considered) is a good case in point. The best example, however, comes a chapter earlier in the Gospel. Jesus, challenging the notion that we should stick up for our rights, supplies us with a well-known proverb:

> You have heard that it was said, "An eye for an eye and a tooth for a tooth." But I say to you, Do not resist one who is evil. But if any one strikes you on the right cheek, turn to him the other also.[1]

Who *does* that?

"Turn the other cheek!" is followed by a string of demands of a similar ilk. If someone drags you to court to take the shirt off your back, let the poor fellow[2] have your jacket as well. If a Roman soldier makes you carry his bags for a mile, offer to carry them for a second (hence the proverbial expression "Go

---

1. Matthew 5:38–39 RSV. The NRSV omits "to him" from its translation, recognizing that Jesus' directive remains the same whether the assailant is male or female. It leaves unstated, however, what Matthew's Greek text specifies, namely, that the "other" cheek is to be turned to the assailant who has already struck the first.

2. Or, of course, "poor woman"; see the preceding note.

the second mile!"). Give to anyone who asks you for something.
Don't turn away from anyone who wants to borrow from you.
Love your enemies. Do good to those who hate you. . . .
Who does *any* of these things?

Nor is this all. If we were to follow Jesus' teaching in the rest of
Matthew 5, we would never insult anyone, swear to anything, or
seek a divorce.[3] Men would tear out their eyes before they would
look at a woman with lust (= sexual desire without love).[4] And
we would all make it a goal to be meek (which, appropriately
enough, rhymes with "weak").[5] Whatever else we may say of
these prescriptions, they are clearly meant for life in a different
world from ours, where the perfect put-down is an art form,
divorce is a growth industry, sex appeal sells everything from
movies to deodorant, and "In your face!" defines the preferred way of treating people with whom we differ. Jesus' demands have always been found difficult. For many today, they seem pointless.

> Not *being* good but having a good time is the principle that steers many of our choices.

Bluntly put, Jesus wants people to be good—and we have at least two problems with the notion. First, *being* good is not a goal most of
us have set for our lives; having a good time—living as long as
possible, with as little pain and as much pleasure as possible—
is the principle that, consciously or unconsciously, steers our
choices. "Turn the other cheek" does not sound like fun: reason
enough, for many of us, not to consider it. Even more basic is
the second problem: what Jesus thinks good, many of us think
crazy. Why would *anyone* "turn the other cheek," "go the second
mile," or flee from occasions of sexual excitement? What makes
any of these things "good"?

Making Sense of Jesus' Demands

How are we to make sense of Jesus' words? Perhaps we may
begin by noting that although they are based on a vision of how

---

3. Matthew 5:21–22, 33–37, 31–32.
4. Matthew 5:28–29.
5. Matthew 5:5.

the world *ought* to look, Jesus' demands do not presuppose that the world as we know it is what it ought to be. Before one can "turn the *other* cheek," one must be struck on the first; in an ideal world, presumably, this would not happen. Nor, in an ideal world, would we find ourselves dealing with foreign soldiers who occupy our country, lawsuits that threaten to take away our shirt, or persecutors to whom we must decide how best to respond. The world in which Jesus tells us to live without worry, without insisting on our rights, but rigorously disciplining our sexual desires, is—in Jesus' own mind—a world whose very nature tempts us to do otherwise: a world, in other words, that in this regard is very much like our own.

What distinguishes Jesus' thinking from our own is thus not that he sees the world as a better place than we think it or that he sees people as better than we know them to be. On the contrary, the Jesus who does not tolerate insults, oaths, impure thoughts, or divorce sees rampant evil ruining everything where we see nothing but the ordinary stuff of life. Nor is Jesus' sense of rampant evil unrelated to his perception that the world is charged with the glory and goodness of God: people with a vision of the good are the ones most readily upset by the appearance of evil. Jesus lives in a world of good and evil—of infinite goodness and unacceptable evil. Lacking his vision of the good, we have difficulty seeing (at least some of) the evil.

> Jesus lives in a world of good and evil—of infinite goodness and unacceptable evil. Lacking his vision of the good, we have difficulty seeing (at least some of) the evil.

Without, then, some sense that our world is not the world as it ought to be, we will never understand the teaching of Jesus. Yet such a sense, at some level at least, we all share. We tend to accept or even admire the telling insult, the pluck of people who stand up for their rights, the cheek of those who get in the face of anyone in their way; and if sex appeal sells everything from movies to deodorant, then those who find such advertisements offensive must be few. But all of us draw lines. Putting people down may be an art form, but killing them is murder. Sticking up for our imagined rights is one thing; going to war to secure them is another. Sexual stimulation may strike us as a good time; but unfaithfulness in a relationship is at least dubious, and rape is certainly wrong. We, too, draw lines. Jesus, we may say, simply draws them much earlier than we tend to do.

Perhaps, then, a way to make sense of his demands is to suggest that a world in which people show contempt for others by insulting them is a world in which some will go on to commit murder; a world in which people are encouraged to stick up for their rights and are admired when they get in others' faces is a world in which war is inevitable; a world in which human sexual appetites are everywhere stimulated will not be without relational unfaithfulness and sexual assault. However unrealistic we may think Jesus' demands, we can at least see the point of trying to prevent the occurrence of obvious wrongs by cutting them off at their roots.

It makes some sense, but not the sense that Jesus is making. No doubt, if we refuse to insult others, we will never dream of murdering them. Jesus' point, however, is that for people who ought to be good as God their Father is good, insulting others is itself unthinkable: insults no less than murder are a sin against goodness.[6] No doubt, if men refused to look at women they encounter with sexual desire, they would never be guilty of marital unfaithfulness or rape. But Jesus' point is that for people who ought to be good as God is good, desiring a woman to whom one is not committed in love is itself sin—and no less a sin against goodness than adultery. (We should rather tear out an eye than be guilty of committing it.)[7]

> Jesus' point is that for people who ought to be good as God their Father is good, insulting others is itself unthinkable: insults no less than murder are a sin against goodness.

The list goes on.[8] In a society in which men could divorce their wives for the slightest cause and show little concern for their welfare, Jesus declares that the marriage covenant should never be broken—because that was God's plan when, to overcome human loneliness and self-centeredness, God instituted mar-

6. Matthew 5:21–22.
7. Matthew 5:27–29.
8. Matthew 5:33–48.

riage.[9] In a society in which people swore constantly that they were telling the truth, Jesus forbids oaths—because calling on God to adjudicate our disputes is irreverent and because swearing that we are *now* telling the truth implies that at other times we need not be as scrupulous. Though we may think retaliation fair provided it does not exceed the initial wrong ("An eye for an eye and a tooth for a tooth"), Jesus tells us to respond to evil with good ("Turn the other cheek"; "Go the second mile," and so forth).[10] Though humans naturally restrict love and kindness to those who reciprocate, Jesus tells us to extend them even to our enemies—as God, in his goodness, sends sunshine and rain on just and unjust alike.

The Goodness of God–in Action

No amount of explanation will make Jesus' demands seem commonplace or even (apart from Jesus' vision of divine goodness) reasonable, but a few explanations may help us put their apparent *un*reasonableness in its proper perspective.

1. Jesus is telling his followers how to behave in a society that is far from ideal; he is not telling rulers how they should legislate. Christians would one day find themselves responsible for shaping society's laws, but this situation is not envisaged in Matthew 5. To this day Christians disagree about how or even whether Jesus' words should affect the decisions of those who legislate or judge. We need not address the issue here but only note that

9. See Matthew 19:3–9, recalling Genesis 2:18–24. The logic by which divorce is said to *lead to* adultery in Matthew 5:32 is that God, who "joined" a married couple together in the first place (Matthew 19:6), does not recognize the divorce that separates them; it follows that one who remarries after a divorce is, in the eyes of One for whom the original marriage remains in force, entering an adulterous relationship. In Jewish law a wife was able to initiate a divorce only in exceptional circumstances; with this in mind, Matthew 5:32 holds the husband who initiates a divorce responsible for the adultery involved in his wife's remarriage *unless* it was her own marital unfaithfulness that precipitated the divorce in the first place.

10. In his letters, the apostle Paul seems to paraphrase Jesus' words in more straightforward terms: "See that none of you repays evil for evil, but always seek to do good to one another and to all" (1 Thessalonians 5:15); "Do not repay anyone evil for evil, but take thought for what is noble in the sight of all. . . . Do not be overcome by evil, but overcome evil with good" (Romans 12:17, 21).

in Matthew 5 Jesus' followers are depicted as a minority group, subject to persecution and abuse but meant to stand out, by the goodness of their behavior, as the world's "salt" and "light."[11]

2. Just as Jesus often tells stories (parables) to convey a point, so he often expresses the requirements of a good life in a dramatic, poetic form that defies literal observance. Tearing out one's eye will not put an end to sexual temptation, nor were Jesus' words intended to suggest that it would. But neither were they meant to be ignored. The drastic picture conveys the point that followers of Jesus must vigilantly avoid foreseeable temptations and rigorously shun them when they arise. "Turn the other cheek" is a graphic way of expressing the demand to respond to evil with a love that, regardless of personal cost, seeks the wrongdoer's best. Matthew's Gospel supplies us with many other examples[12] of demands whose literal fulfillment would lead to absurdity but whose spirit must be practiced by any who would claim to be Jesus' disciple.[13]

3. The peculiar nature of Jesus' demands corresponds to his understanding of goodness. Straightforward laws they are not. The latter, in telling us precisely what to do and precisely what we will suffer if we fail to do so, may restrain wrongdoing[14] and guide us to live by principles rather than by whims or passions. But true, deep-down goodness is never a matter of mere compliance with laws. Deep-down goodness shows itself in spontaneous generosity, uncalculating kindness, and unstinted love.[15] It is related to joy, thankfulness, and appreciativeness—though none of these qualities necessarily accompanies the most strenuous efforts for self-discipline and moral virtue. True goodness is itself inspired by a vision of goodness: in Jesus' case, a vision of the goodness of God and of life in his care. It is the goodness of those

11. Matthew 5:10–12, 39, 44, 13–16.

12. For example, Matthew 6:3: "When you give alms, do not let your left hand know what your right hand is doing"; 6:6: "Whenever you pray, go into your room and shut the door and pray to your Father who is in secret"; 7:5: "First take the log out of your own eye, and then you will see clearly to take the speck out of your neighbor's eye"; 7:6: "Do not throw your pearls before swine."

13. See Matthew 7:21–27; 28:19–20.

14. Jesus shows himself aware of this dimension of their purpose in Matthew 19:7–8.

15. Note the ideal of self-forgetfulness in kindness reflected in Matthew 6:3; 25:37–40.

who know themselves to be children of a benevolent Creator and who want to be like their heavenly Father. If Jesus' demands are framed more poetically than legally, it is because poetry evokes a vision; and Jesus' demands can only be met by those who have been captured by a vision and live in its light.

> True, deep-down goodness is never a matter of mere compliance with laws. Deep-down goodness shows itself in spontaneous generosity, uncalculating kindness, and unstinted love. It is itself inspired by a vision of goodness.

4. Just as such goodness is not the product of resolutions to try harder, be a better person, live up to one's principles, or obey others' laws, so it is not first aggrieved when laws are transgressed. Laws are not violated but goodness is when we put down others with cutting insults or look on them as mere means to our own sexual gratification. The issue for Jesus is not at what point we draw the line between acceptable and unacceptable evil but whether we side with the goodness of God or with the evil that opposes it.

5. There is nothing calculating about the goodness Jesus requires. Jesus forbids insults and looks of lust because they are wrong, not because such prohibitions may at least serve to reduce instances of murder and marital unfaithfulness. Jesus commands his disciples to treat with kindness those who abuse them because such is the goodness of God, not because kind actions are likely to disarm opponents and turn them into friends. Jesus nowhere suggests that, by our little deeds of kindness, we can make the world a better place;[16] he tells us how we must live if we acknowledge God as our Father.

6. What makes good the things that Jesus considers good? For Jesus, what is good for human beings is defined by the nature and purposes of God who created them. Insults that express contempt for people whom God has created can never be good. Sexual drives serve the end for which they were created when they prod us to commit ourselves to another in love and when, within the boundaries of committed love, they find expression in acts of pro-

---

16. He does, however, have much to say about how the world will be transformed into a better place. We will consider his vision of the kingdom of heaven in subsequent chapters.

creation that both cement the relationship and give birth to others whom we shelter and love.[17] Humans are thus called to enjoy their sexuality as partners of their Creator, promoting the perpetuation and well-being of their race.[18] Conversely, when detached from its relation-enhancing and procreative purposes, human sexuality is reduced to a sterile pursuit of self-gratification. If marriage, as Jesus believes, has been instituted by God for humanity's well-being, then withdrawing from its commitments means tearing apart what God, for our good, has joined together. The climate of irreverence and allowable falsehoods perpetuated by oaths does not suit a world governed by the goodness of God. Sticking up for one's rights is absurd for people who claim the Lord of the universe as their Father, and it runs counter to God's purpose to overcome evil with good. Similarly, children of the Almighty should hardly feel threatened when people oppose them; they can afford to be magnanimous, as God their Father is magnanimous.

> The issue for Jesus is not at what point we draw the line between acceptable and unacceptable evil but whether we side with the goodness of God or with the evil that opposes it.

7. If Jesus sees evil where many today see none (insults, lust, divorce, oaths), he also portrays God as extending to his children unlimited forgiveness. Jesus' demands, as Matthew records them, may seem ridiculously beyond what real people can achieve; yet

17. Note what Genesis 1:27–28 and 2:18, 23–24 imply about God's purposes in creating humankind as "male and female."

18. The point is captured beautifully in a sermon Bonhoeffer prepared in prison for the wedding of his best friend to his niece:

> Marriage is more than your love for each other. It has a higher dignity and power, for it is God's holy ordinance, through which he wills to perpetuate the human race till the end of time. In your love you see only your two selves in the world, but in marriage you are a link in the chain of the generations, which God causes to come and to pass away to his glory, and calls into his kingdom. In your love you see only the heaven of your own happiness, but in marriage you are placed at a post of responsibility towards the world and mankind. Your love is your own private possession, but marriage is more than something personal—it is a status, an office. Just as it is the crown, and not merely the will to rule, that makes the king, so it is marriage, and not merely your love for each other, that joins you together in the sight of God and man. . . . It is not your love that sustains the marriage, but from now on, the marriage that sustains your love. (Dietrich Bonhoeffer, *Letters and Papers from Prison*, ed. Eberhard Bethge, expanded ed. [New York: Simon & Schuster, 1997], 42–43)

it is real people for whom the Jesus of Matthew's Gospel shows an obvious love and with whose failures he shows unending patience. He seeks out the company of society's most notorious "sinners."[19] He surrounds himself with disciples consistent only in their shortcomings and promises them God's forgiveness as long as they forgive others.[20] He illustrates the point with a parable

> Jesus' demands may seem ridiculously beyond what real people can achieve; yet it is real people for whom the Jesus of Matthew's Gospel shows an obvious love and with whose failures he shows unending patience.

of a servant who refused to overlook a fellow-servant's trivial debt although he himself had been forgiven an enormous sum.[21] All of us, by implication, require an enormous amount of forgiveness, and God (Jesus says) is willing to grant it—provided we are willing to live as God's children. Forgiveness is denied only to those who refuse to let the goodness of God shape their own response to their fellow human beings.

A Disciple in Evil Times

Matthew's Gospel may be full of demands that many people know and few set out to follow, but Dietrich Bonhoeffer was definitely among the latter. Even in a book devoted to understanding Matthew, we may pause for a moment to consider the extraordinary story of one man's attempt to apply its vision to life in perilous times.

From the earliest days of Nazi power, Bonhoeffer was a vocal and fearless critic, a "fanatic" and "radical" in the eyes of many. But thanks to his brother-in-law, Hans von Dohnanyi, Bonhoeffer was better informed than most of Nazi atrocities. Dohnanyi, who worked first in the German Ministry of Justice and later in the Military Intelligence Office, kept a secret journal, a "chronicle of shame," that documented the criminal actions of Nazi party leaders. It included stories of the concentration camps, of the

---

19. Matthew 9:10–13; 11:19.
20. Matthew 6:12, 14–15.
21. Matthew 18:21–35.

treatment of prisoners of war, and of the pogroms against the Jews. Dohnanyi also introduced Bonhoeffer to the circle of conspirators to which he belonged, a group determined to put an end to the Nazi regime. Initially they plotted to arrest Hitler and put him on trial. When those plans were frustrated, they concluded that their only recourse was to assassinate him. At several points they nearly succeeded; but they never did, and the dramatic failure of July 20, 1944, cost the conspirators their lives.

> Bonhoeffer joined a group of conspirators who plotted to assassinate Hitler. Under the circumstances, he believed this was the only responsible thing to do.

Bonhoeffer joined the group, believing that, under the circumstances, this was the only responsible course of action for him to take. Responsible action could not mean reasoning with Hitler; that was utter naïveté. It did not mean (Bonhoeffer came to realize) raising one's voice in moral indignation; protests changed nothing but served only to salve the conscience of the protester. Nor could responsible action mean dutifully doing what one was told to do: German "submissiveness and self-sacrifice" were now being "exploited for evil ends."[22] And it could not mean turning one's back on all that was happening and retreating into a sanctuary of private virtue: only by shutting one's eyes and mouth to injustice could one imagine oneself pure.[23] For Bonhoeffer, God's call to responsible action meant plotting to kill the "tyrannical despiser of humanity"[24]—and, necessarily, covering one's activities and those of one's co-conspirators with lies and deception.

Many ethicists would find Bonhoeffer's course of action entirely justified on moral grounds. In normal times one has an obligation to submit to the government and tell the truth; but conditions in Germany of the 1930s were not normal, and the Nazi regime had abused its power. Under *these* circumstances, many would argue, one's foremost duty becomes to subvert and end such a government. In this view, Bonhoeffer and his fellow conspirators were simply fulfilling their duty and incurred no guilt in plotting against Hitler.

22. Bonhoeffer, *Letters and Papers*, 6.
23. Ibid., 4–5; also 298.
24. Dietrich Bonhoeffer, *Ethics* (Minneapolis: Fortress, 2005), 85.

Bonhoeffer himself saw the matter differently. It *was* wrong to lie, it *was* wrong to kill, but protecting one's "innocence"—keeping one's hands "clean"—by doing nothing while the Nazis murdered any whom they deemed undesirable was simply not an option. Plotting to kill and lying to cover one's activities meant, on one level, breaking not only the laws of society but also the Ten Commandments and the Sermon on the Mount; still, faithfulness to God required it. To promote the good of others, one had to be prepared to assume guilt oneself.[25]

> To promote the good of others, one had to be prepared to assume guilt oneself.

Bonhoeffer took seriously the notion that he and his co-conspirators were doing wrong. He knew their actions would be judged harshly by many within the church, and wondered whether, if he survived the war, he would be allowed to hold church office. Indeed, he wondered whether people who had so sullied their innocence could be of any use in the restoration of community that would one day be necessary—when the war was over and the tyrants overthrown.[26] But the task for the moment, regardless of these considerations, was to get rid of Hitler. His decision to proceed was based on at least the following three considerations.

1. A sharp distinction should be drawn, Bonhoeffer believed, between adopting lawlessness as a pattern of living and transgressing the law when such action seems unavoidable if just law is to be restored.[27] "Certainly no responsible activity is possible that does not consider with ultimate seriousness the boundary that God established in the law." Any

---

25. Put differently, responsibility meant, for Bonhoeffer, not playing the solitary hero but doing his part to make the world fit for coming generations: "The ultimate question for a responsible man to ask is not how he is to extricate himself heroically from the affair, but how the coming generation is to live" (*Letters and Papers*, 7).

26. "We have been silent witnesses of evil deeds; we have been drenched by many storms; we have learnt the arts of equivocation and pretence; experience has made us suspicious of others and kept us from being truthful and open; intolerable conflicts have worn us down and even made us cynical. Are we still of any use? What we shall need is not geniuses, or cynics, or misanthropes, or clever tacticians, but plain, honest, straightforward men. Will our inward power of resistance be strong enough, and our honesty with ourselves remorseless enough, for us to find our way back to simplicity and straightforwardness?" (ibid., 16–17).

27. Ibid., 10–11.

suspension of the law must only serve its true fulfillment. In war, for example, there is killing, lying, and seizing of property solely in order to reinstate the validity of life, truth, and property. Breaking the law must be *recognized* in all its gravity. . . . Whether an action springs from responsibility or cynicism can become evident only in whether the objective guilt one incurs by breaking the law is recognized and borne, and whether by the very act of breaking it the law is truly sanctified.[28]

2. What we have seen so far might easily be confused with the conventional wisdom that evil times demand unusual measures. Bonhoeffer's own thinking, however, was closely linked to his understanding of the gospel. We cannot pause here for even the most rudimentary summary of his *Ethics*. Still, something must be said of the connection he saw between responsible action and life as a follower of Jesus.

For Bonhoeffer, ethics is a preoccupation for a humanity that has lost its innocence. Only because we are not governed by delight in God and love for others are we continually beset by questions of good and evil: knowledge of good and evil is itself a consequence of sin.[29] And Jesus is fundamentally misunderstood when his mission is thought to lie in bringing a new ethical program, in supplying new (perhaps more rigid) criteria for distinguishing good from evil. Not even the Sermon on the Mount is an ethical program.[30] Jesus came to redeem the world, not to recalibrate its moral codes.[31] His own life was devoted not to cultivating personal virtue or embodying ethical principles but to acting responsibly in the world in the service of God and others. Followers of Jesus, then, cannot abandon engagement with the world in order to realize some ethical ideal.[32] Not even when they love others are they pursuing an ethical principle;

28. Bonhoeffer, *Ethics*, 297; see also 234–35.

29. Ibid., 299–300; see Genesis 2:17; 3:1–6.

30. Bonhoeffer, *Ethics*, 229–31.

31. "Since Jesus Christ is the incarnate love of God for human beings, he is not the proclaimer of abstract ethical ideologies, but the one who concretely enacts God's love" (ibid., 232).

32. "The Sermon on the Mount itself confronts a person with the necessity of responsible historical action. . . . It calls individuals to love, which proves itself in responsible action toward the neighbor and whose source is the love of God that encompasses all of reality" (ibid., 242–43).

rather, they are participating in God's world-reconciling love.[33] And since Jesus, in love, took upon himself the guilt of the world, they need not hesitate, in love, to take on themselves the guilt with which the world is burdened.[34] "Love for real human beings leads into the solidarity of human guilt."[35]

3. For Bonhoeffer, both the judgment and the consequences of responsible action must be left to God.[37] Those who "deliver their action into God's hands" have to "console themselves with faith in the forgiving and healing grace of God."[38]

> "Christ did not, like an ethicist, love a theory about the good; he loved real people."[36]

Whatever else we may learn from Bonhoeffer, it is certainly true that, for Matthew, Jesus' teaching cannot be isolated from his broader mission: in Jesus' deeds as well as his words, his destiny as well as his activities, the "kingdom of heaven" draws "near." To the background and content of this mission we must now turn.

---

33. "Love—as understood in the gospel in contrast to all philosophy—is not a method for dealing with people. Instead, it is the reality of being drawn and drawing others into an event, namely, into God's community with the world, which has already been accomplished in Jesus Christ" (ibid., 241).

34. "God wills to be guilty of our guilt; God takes on the punishment and suffering that guilt has brought on us. God takes responsibility for godlessness, love for hate, the holy one for the sinner. Now there is no more godlessness, hate, or sin that God has not taken upon himself, suffered, and atoned. Now there is no longer any reality, any world, that is not reconciled with God and at peace. God has done this in the beloved son, Jesus Christ" (ibid., 83; also 233–34). See the discussion in chapter 5, below, under the heading "The Cross and the Kingdom."

35. Bonhoeffer, *Ethics*, 233.

36. Ibid., 98.

37. Ibid., 225.

38. Ibid., 227.

4

Dialogue
with the Almighty

In everyone's life there is a story. Blessed with the gift of memory, we recall the past, and it shapes how we see ourselves today. Blessed with the gift of imagination, we picture life as we would like it and shape our plans accordingly. Unable to control our circumstances and sharing space with other human beings who have plans of their own, we often find our purposes thwarted, our hopes unfulfilled. In making and pursuing plans and in reacting to their achievement or frustration, our character is formed, and character has its own role in shaping our activities. Different pasts, different plans, different circumstances, and different characters combine to make every human life unique, with its own distinctive story.

That story begins long before our birth. We grow up under the influence of parents and others whose influence on our lives has in turn been shaped by the influence of earlier generations. Long after our deaths, our influence continues on those with whom we lived and affects the influence they have on succeeding generations. Our own distinctive stories are thus an inextricable part of a chain of events that goes back at least as far as human beginnings on earth and will continue as long as the race endures: humankind, too, has its story.

How we understand our own story depends in large measure on how we understand the story of humankind as a whole: where we have come from, how we reached where we are, where we are headed. Barney and Bernie (people, that is, with differing worldviews) will see these matters very differently.[1] Barney, typically, will see any pattern in his life as the product either of his own designs or of fortuitous circumstances ("as luck would have it"). Bernie, like Shakespeare's Hamlet, is likely to believe

> There's a divinity that shapes our ends,
> Rough-hew them how we will.[2]

Jews such as Jesus (and Matthew) believed that human life takes on its decisive shape by the appropriateness or inappropriateness of our responses to God, the giver and sustainer of life. But they also believed that the God who created us is no passive observer of human affairs. Jews saw themselves engaged, throughout their lives and throughout the history of their people, in the give-and-take of a dialogue with the Almighty. And a *dialogue* it was: Israel was no docile partner. If at times God and Israel exchanged sweet words of love, at other times their debates were heated, their accusations bitter, and reproaches led to a parting of the ways. Yet the partings were always temporary; however volatile the relationship, the attachment proved too deep to be lastingly severed. There was something special about God and Israel.

> Jews saw themselves engaged, throughout their lives and throughout the history of their people, in the give-and-take of a dialogue with the Almighty. And Israel was no docile partner in this dialogue.

That history, Jesus and Matthew both believed, reached a climactic moment when Jesus began his public activities. Before we explore the climax, however, we must remind ourselves briefly of the story that preceded it. This chapter will focus on

---

1. See chapter 1, above.
2. William Shakespeare, *Hamlet*, 5.2.10–11; that is, God keeps our lives on track in spite of the mess we make of things.

four moments in Israel's past that shaped Jesus' (and Matthew's) understanding of their present. Matthew himself supplies us with three of them in the opening chapter of his Gospel: he divides Jesus' genealogy into three segments, conveying the message that the story of Jesus, like those of Abraham, David, and the Babylonian exile before him, marks a significant moment in Israel's history. Moses does not figure in the list: born into a different Israelite tribe, he could hardly appear in Jesus' genealogy. But echoes of Moses' story dominate the early chapters of Matthew's Gospel and recur at important points in the later narrative as well. To understand Jesus as Matthew understood him, we must know something about Moses also.

> For Matthew, the story of Jesus, like those of Abraham, David, and the Babylonian exile before him, marks a significant moment in Israel's history.

Abraham

Matthew begins Jesus' genealogy at the point where Israel's story itself began, with Abraham. Like our own, his knowledge of Abraham was derived, directly and indirectly, from Genesis, the first book of the Jews' sacred scriptures. Abraham (or Abram, as he is initially called) left Ur of the Chaldeans for Haran in northern Mesopotamia, then left Haran for Canaan in response to the summons that launched the dialogue between the Almighty and Israel:

Go from your country and your kindred and your father's house to the land that I will show you. I will make of you a great nation, and I will bless you, and make your name great, so that you will be a blessing. I will bless those who bless you, and the one who curses you I will curse; and in you all the families of the earth shall be blessed.[3]

---

3. Genesis 12:1–3. The last words of the quotation may also be translated, "By you all the families of the earth shall bless themselves" (see the alternate translation given in the NRSV); that is, they will regard Abraham as the standard of blessing and wish themselves as blessed as he is. The Old Greek translation, however, understood Genesis 12:3 as saying that all nations would be blessed through Abraham (see also

Genesis itself does not begin with Abraham but with the insistence that all human beings are God's creatures, living in the world God created.[4] Yet in the Genesis account we prove to be wayward creatures indeed: rather than trust our Creator, we follow our own judgment of what serves our interests; we quickly fill the world with violence; our hearts are inclined toward evil from our youth; we devise ways to make a name for ourselves apart from God.[5] The call of Abraham appears in Genesis as God's response to the human catastrophe: unwilling to give up on his creation, God enters a formal relationship (a "covenant") with Abraham and his offspring. He will be their God, and they will be his people. And he will make of them an object lesson for the nations, displaying through Israel his goodness.

> The call of Abraham appears in Genesis as God's response to the human catastrophe: unwilling to give up on his creation, God enters a covenant with Abraham and his offspring. He will be their God, and they will be his people.

Apart from his mention in Jesus' genealogy, Abraham scarcely appears in Matthew's Gospel. On the other hand, the distinction between descendants of Abraham (Israel, or the Jewish people) and other nations (the Gentiles) is crucial to the narrative. We may briefly note four aspects of its depiction.

1. Jesus' own mission, and that of his disciples in the course of the Gospel, is devoted to Israel. Of himself Jesus says, "I was sent only to the lost sheep of the house of Israel."[6] Changing the metaphor, he says that he often "desired to gather [Jerusalem's] children together as a hen gathers her brood under her wings."[7] To his disciples he gives the charge "Go nowhere among the Gentiles, and enter no town of the Samaritans, but go rather to the lost sheep of the house of Israel. As you go, proclaim the good news, 'The kingdom of heaven has come near.'"[8] The end of the latter quotation introduces the content of Jesus' mission; this will concern

---

Galatians 3:8). For the notion that Israel is a source of blessing for the Gentile nations, see also Isaiah 2:3; 60:1–3.

4. See Genesis 1.
5. Genesis 3:1–6; 6:11; 8:21; 11:4.
6. Matthew 15:24.
7. Matthew 23:37.
8. Matthew 10:5–7.

us in due course. For the moment we note only that in Matthew's Gospel Jesus advances the agenda announced by God to Abraham, focusing his activities on God's covenant people, Israel.

2. Israel's relationship with God was never smooth; in Matthew the complications continue. On the positive side of the ledger, we may note that Jesus' own disciples were Jews. Moreover, crowds of Jews often seem sympathetic to Jesus and his mission;[9] certainly they come to Jesus for help.[10] On the other hand, Jesus' predecessor John the Baptist charges his fellow countrymen with presuming that as Abraham's children, they were assured of God's favor regardless of their (sinful) deeds.[11] Jesus announces that although Israel's forefathers (Abraham, Isaac, and Jacob) will have an honored place in God's kingdom, descendants of theirs will find themselves banished to "the outer darkness."[12] When he speaks of his desire to gather Jerusalem's children as a hen gathers her brood to protect them, he notes that his efforts have been thwarted: "You were not willing."[13] "This generation" of Jews (or "this evil generation")[14] is said to perpetuate and exceed the sins of their forefathers and to face the brunt of divine judgment for their ancestors' wrongdoing as well as their own.[15] Even Gentile cities notorious in Scripture for their corruption will encounter more leniency at God's last judgment than unrepentant Israel.[16]

> In Matthew's Gospel, Jesus advances the agenda announced by God to Abraham, focusing his activities on God's covenant people, Israel.

3. Matthew's Jesus devotes his attention to Israel; still, the ultimate beneficiaries of his mission include people of all nations. At times Gentiles appear in Matthew's Gospel in their accustomed role as outsiders who show no grasp of how to approach God and only minimal standards of decency in relating to each other.[17]

---

9. For example, Matthew 4:25; 7:28–29; 9:8, 33; 12:15, 23.
10. For example, Matthew 4:24; 8:16; 9:2; 12:22.
11. Matthew 3:8–10.
12. Matthew 8:11–12.
13. Matthew 23:37.
14. Matthew 12:39, 41–42, 45; compare 16:4; 17:17.
15. Matthew 23:34–36.
16. Matthew 10:14–15; 11:20–24; see also 12:41–42.
17. Matthew 5:47; 6:7; 10:5; 18:17.

Elsewhere, however, there are encouraging signs. Women with non-Israelite connections (Tamar, Rahab, Ruth, and "the wife of Uriah") seem to be singled out for attention in Jesus' genealogy.[18] No Jews honor Jesus at his birth in Matthew's Gospel, but "wise men from the East . . . come to pay him homage."[19] Jesus praises a Roman centurion for demonstrating greater faith than anything he found in Israel;[20] he commends a Canaanite woman for the greatness of her faith;[21] and he is acknowledged to be God's Son at his death by another Roman centurion.[22] The Gospel makes clear at several points that the restriction of Jesus' message to a Jewish audience is only temporary,[23] and it concludes with a commission to make disciples of "all nations."[24]

> Matthew's Jesus devotes his attention to Israel; still, the ultimate beneficiaries of his mission include people of all nations.

4. It has sometimes been suggested that Matthew has written off the Jewish people, that he considers them to have forfeited their prerogatives as the people of God and to have been replaced by Gentile followers of Jesus. Clearly, as just noted, Matthew believes that judgment looms over the unrepentant in Israel; just as clearly he portrays the kingdom of God as open to people of all nations who respond to the gospel. It does not follow, however, that he thinks Jews have been, or should be, abandoned as a lost cause. The latter interpretation goes beyond the texts cited in its support and runs counter to too much evidence in the Gospel to be tenable.

a. Matthew 21:43 does say that "the kingdom of God will be taken away from you and given to a people that produces the fruits of the kingdom." But the target of Jesus' words is then identified not as the Jewish people but as the "chief priests and the Pharisees."[25] Portrayed as tenants in charge of a vineyard who fail to turn over its fruit, Israel's leaders are accused of exploiting

18. Matthew 1:3, 5–6.
19. Matthew 2:1–2.
20. Matthew 8:10.
21. Matthew 15:21–28.
22. Matthew 27:54.
23. Matthew 10:18; 24:9, 14; 26:13.
24. Matthew 28:19.
25. Matthew 21:45.

their mandate for selfish ends. But the punishment of tenants need not mean the destruction of the vineyard.[26]

b. In Matthew's account of Jesus' trial, the Jewish people take upon themselves responsibility for his death: "His blood be on us and on our children!"[27] These are horrible words, and Matthew thought them horribly true to events a generation later when the Romans destroyed Jerusalem and massacred Jews by the thousands. It scarcely follows that Matthew thought Jews, beyond that judgment, remained an accursed people.[28]

> A strange Messiah Jesus would be indeed if Jews have no part in his kingdom—and he could not be their king.

c. Matthew clearly expected that the mission of Jesus' disciples to the Jews would continue until the end of the age.[29] Indeed, he indicates that Jews would one day welcome Jesus' return.[30]

d. If Jesus was to emerge from Bethlehem as the one who would "shepherd my [God's] people Israel," then Israel remains God's people.[31] In a similar vein, Matthew is convinced that Jesus is the Messiah, a title he equates with "king of the Jews."[32] A strange Messiah he would be indeed if Jews have no part in his kingdom—and he could not be their king.

Moses

After much drama, the aged Abraham and his almost equally aged wife Sarah have a son, Isaac, through whom God's promises

---

26. Matthew 21:33–45.

27. Matthew 27:25.

28. The idea that the Roman destruction of Jerusalem (like its destruction centuries earlier by the Babylonians) represented a divine judgment for specifiable wrongs was widespread among Jews. That, beyond judgment, God would return in favor to his people was the usual sequel.

29. Matthew 10:23.

30. Matthew 23:39. Note, too, that Matthew 19:28 envisages Israel's continued existence (as twelve tribes) at the time of "the renewal of all things": they will then be governed by Jesus' disciples.

31. Matthew 2:6. Note that God, for Matthew, remains "the God of Israel" (15:31).

32. Matthew 2:1–6; see also 21:5. The notion that Jesus is Messiah will be treated later in this chapter.

to Abraham's descendants can begin to be fulfilled.[33] After a love story more typical of the ancient (or non-Western) world than our own, Isaac marries Rebekah, who gives birth to twins, Esau and Jacob.[34] After one of the most famous fraternal disputes in the pages of literature or the scripts of recent musicals, Jacob and eleven sons join Joseph in Egypt.[35] In the course of time, their descendants become slaves of the Egyptians.[36]

It is through Moses that God delivers his people from their Egyptian bondage.[37] And it is through Moses, on Mount Sinai, that God gives Israel the laws they are to observe as his covenant people. The Ten Commandments are the most famous part of this legislation.[38] But included as well are laws both civil and criminal and a host of prescriptions for the food Israelites are to eat, ceremonial washings they are to observe, festivals they are to celebrate, dues they are to collect, sacrifices they are to offer, and so on. It should also be remembered that the generation that Moses led out of Egypt is notorious in Israelite history for its discontent, its rebelliousness, and its periodic episodes of idolatry and immorality. Eventually "that generation," "loathed" by God,[39] is doomed to perish in the wilderness.[40]

> More than any other Gospel writer, Matthew wants us to see parallels between Moses and Jesus.

Moses matters much to Matthew. Here we can only note a few of the incidents in the Gospel that recall stories of Moses and comment briefly on how the Jesus of Matthew's Gospel regards the Mosaic law.

1. *Echoes of Moses.* More than any other Gospel writer, Matthew wants us to see parallels between Moses and Jesus. Here are a few obvious examples.

a. At his birth Moses barely escapes death at the hands of a wicked ruler who attempts to kill Israelite baby boys. Baby

---

33. Genesis 21:1–7.
34. Genesis 24:1–67; 25:19–26.
35. Genesis 37:1–47:28.
36. Exodus 1:8–14.
37. Exodus 3:1–12:51; see also 14:1–31.
38. Exodus 20:1–17.
39. Psalm 95:10.
40. God's commands to Israel and the story of the wilderness generation are found in Exodus 20–40 and the books of Leviticus, Numbers, and Deuteronomy.

Jesus, too, barely escapes death at the hands of Herod, who kills all infant boys in the vicinity of Bethlehem.[41]

b. Both Moses and Jesus spend parts of their early life in Egypt.[42]

c. Moses, whose life is sought by Pharaoh, keeps out of his reach until God tells him, "All those who were seeking your life are dead." Jesus, whose life is sought by Herod, is kept out of his reach until an angel tells Joseph, "Those who were seeking the child's life are dead."[43]

d. Israel itself, at the time of Moses, was "called" by God "out of Egypt." Matthew applies the same words to Jesus: "Out of Egypt I [God] have called my son."[44]

e. When Moses was with the Lord on Mount Sinai (or Horeb), he fasted for "forty days and forty nights." Jesus, Matthew tells us, was led by God's Spirit into the wilderness, where he fasted for "forty days and forty nights."[45]

f. The Israelites, led by Moses into the wilderness, found themselves hungry and complained against God; at a time of crisis they "put God to the test," demanding that he prove himself God by intervening on their behalf; and they succumbed periodically to idolatry. Jesus, hungry in the wilderness, was tempted to abandon his trust in God; he was challenged to put God to the test by forcing God to intervene on his behalf; and he was offered the world if he would engage in idolatrous worship. Unlike Israel, however, Jesus refused each temptation, quoting words of Moses as he did so.[46]

g. Moses received God's laws on a mountain and communicated them to God's people. Matthew's Jesus instructed his disciples on a mountain.[47]

What does Matthew want us to see in these parallels? If Matthew's Jesus advances the agenda announced by God to Abraham,

41. Exodus 1:22–2:10; Matthew 2:13–18.
42. Exodus 2:1–15; Matthew 2:14–15.
43. Exodus 4:19; Matthew 2:20.
44. Matthew 2:15, quoting Hosea 11:1.
45. Exodus 34:28; Deuteronomy 9:8–9, 18; Matthew 4:1–2.
46. Exodus 16:3, 6–8; 17:1–7; 32:1–6; Matthew 4:1–11.
47. Deuteronomy 9:9–10; Matthew 5–7 (the Sermon on the Mount).

the parallels with Moses reinforce the notion that God's dealings with Israel continue in Jesus' activities. But they continue with a difference: with Jesus things are put right that had earlier gone wrong. Whereas Israel proved unfaithful at the time of Moses, Jesus stood the test.

2. *Jesus and the law of Moses.* In matters of law, however, Jesus' continuity with Moses comes sharply into question. Repeatedly, Matthew tells us, Jesus or his disciples are accused of acting unlawfully. Matthew himself sees the matter differently: at stake for him is the law's true interpretation. Jesus both affirms and fulfills the Mosaic law, when it is rightly understood.

In the Sermon on the Mount (Matthew 5–7) Jesus addresses the perception that he sets aside the law: "Do not think that I have come to abolish the law or the prophets; I have come not to abolish but to fulfill."[48] If the goal of Moses' law is right behavior, Jesus "fulfills" the purpose that underlies the law by spelling out more fully what right behavior entails.[49] Of course, one must avoid acts of murder and adultery, as the law prescribes; but insulting words and lustful looks are themselves sins against God's goodness. The Mosaic law may have permitted divorce, oaths, and measured retribution to avoid even greater evils. But those who would model their conduct after the goodness of God will avoid all three. And they will extend the circle of those they love from "neighbors" (as the law commands) to include even their enemies.

> Jesus, Matthew assures us, both affirms and fulfills the Mosaic law, when it is rightly understood.

Loving God with all our being and a love that shows others the consideration we naturally give to ourselves are, Jesus declares, what the law is all about.[50] The essence of "the law and the prophets" can be summed up in the maxim "Do to others as you would have them do to you."[51] Such summaries of the Mosaic law might seem to overlook a number of its details; and indeed, Jesus does distinguish between the "weightier matters of the law" ("justice and mercy and faith") and lesser subjects (the tithing,

48. Matthew 5:17.

49. The examples that immediately follow (drawn from Matthew 5:21–48) are discussed more fully in chapter 3, above.

50. Matthew 22:34–40.

51. Matthew 7:12.

for example, of "mint, dill, and cummin").[52] The latter demands, too, have their place,[53] but Jesus never presses their observance on his followers, believing that God is more concerned about "mercy" than "sacrifice" (that is, about deeds of compassion rather than prescribed religious duties).[54] To charges of unlawful behavior, Jesus responds by insisting that acts of compassion take precedence over the punctilious observance of legal requirements.[55]

> Loving God with all our being and a love that shows others the consideration we naturally give to ourselves are, for Matthew's Jesus, what the law is all about.

David

For Matthew, Jesus is a descendant of Abraham, and his mission advances the agenda announced in God's covenant with the patriarch. Jesus' story recalls the life of Moses, and Jesus is the true interpreter of Moses' law. Jesus is also, Matthew believes, the "son of David"—and David's "Lord."

As the story unfolds in the Jewish scriptures, the children of the Israelites whom Moses brought out of Egypt are led by Joshua into the land promised to their forebears.[56] Beset by enemies, they in time ask for a king.[57] Saul is chosen for the task but proves unworthy.[58] He is replaced by David, whom God declares to be "a man after his own heart."[59] To David God promises a dynasty that will last forever.

> When your days are fulfilled and you lie down with your ancestors, I will raise up your offspring after you, who shall come forth from your body, and I will establish his kingdom. He shall build a house for my name, and I will establish the throne of his kingdom forever. I will be a father to him, and he shall be a son to me. When he commits iniquity, I will punish him with a rod such as mortals use, with blows

52. Matthew 23:23.
53. Matthew 5:19; 23:23.
54. Matthew 9:13; 12:7.
55. Matthew 12:1–13; see also 9:10–13; 15:1–20.
56. Joshua 1–11.
57. 1 Samuel 8:4–22.
58. 1 Samuel 9:1–15:35.
59. 1 Samuel 13:14.

inflicted by human beings. But I will not take my steadfast love from him, as I took it from Saul, whom I put away from before you. Your house and your kingdom shall be made sure forever before me; your throne shall be established forever.[60]

The dynasty lasted about four centuries. Its demise was pronounced by prophets of the Lord, who found David's descendants unfit to be kings; it was effected by Nebuchadnezzar, king of Babylon, in 586 BCE. A divine commitment, however, cannot come to nothing. If the unfaithfulness of successive descendants of David interrupted the keeping of God's promise, that promise would one day find a still greater fulfillment in a faithful son of David, whose rule would be marked by justice, peace, and prosperity.[61]

> To David God promised a dynasty that would last forever. If the unfaithfulness of successive descendants of David interrupted the keeping of God's promise, that promise would one day find a still greater fulfillment in a faithful son of David, whose rule would be marked by justice, peace, and prosperity.

Jews before, during, and after the days of Jesus longed, and continue to long, for the appearance of such a Messiah (= "anointed" king). Yet in Jesus, Matthew insists, Israel's messianic hopes have found their fulfillment.[62] As the Messiah (Greek *Christos*), Jesus is the "king of the Jews," the "ruler who is to shepherd my [God's] people Israel."[63] If God promised to be a father to kings descended from David,[64] then Jesus is "the Messiah, the Son of the living God."[65] Repeatedly he is approached as the "Son of David,"[66] and as such he is welcomed by crowds headed for Jerusalem: "Hosanna to the Son of David!"[67]

60. 2 Samuel 7:12–16.
61. See, for example, Isaiah 9:6–7; 11:1–9; Jeremiah 23:5–6.
62. Matthew 1:1, 17, 18; 16:13–20, and elsewhere.
63. Matthew 2:2–6.
64. 2 Samuel 7:14.
65. Matthew 16:16; see also 26:63.
66. Matthew 9:27; 15:22; 20:30–31; see also 12:23. It seems likely that Jewish traditions attributing healing powers to David's son Solomon are also reflected in these texts.
67. Matthew 21:9, 15.

We must postpone for later discussion the nature of God's "reign" as inaugurated by Jesus. Two other observations on Jesus' relationship with David are nonetheless in order here.

1. The biblical book of Psalms was traditionally ascribed to David. When in Psalm 110 the writer distinguishes between *"the* Lord" (God) and *"my* Lord" and speaks of the latter as reigning at God's "right hand" (as God's agent, acting on God's behalf), Jesus sees this as David referring to the coming messianic ruler.

> Jesus asked [the Pharisees] this question: "What do you think of the Messiah? Whose son is he?" They said to him, "The son of David." He said to them, "How is it then that David by the Spirit calls him Lord, saying,
>> 'The Lord said to my Lord,
>> "Sit at my right hand,
>>> until I put your enemies under your feet"'?
> If David thus calls him Lord, how can he be his son?"[68]

The text might seem to suggest that the Messiah (Jesus) is *not* the "Son of David" after all; but this cannot be the point, since Matthew, from the first verse of his Gospel, has affirmed that he is. This passage at least insists, however, that "David's son" does not exhaust what needs to be said about Jesus' identity.[69]

2. Since the book of Psalms was attributed to David, psalms of lament were thought to reflect David's own troubles. And just as, for Matthew, much of Moses' story is recapitulated in the life of Jesus, so the sufferings of David, Matthew believes, are relived by David's greater son. Repeatedly the opening chapters of the Gospel echo the biblical narrative of Moses; repeatedly Matthew's account of Jesus' final suffering echoes the biblical book of Psalms. Jesus is betrayed by a trusted friend, as David was betrayed.[70] He is given gall by his foes to drink, as the psalmist also was given.[71] People cast lots for Jesus' clothes, as they did for the psalmist's.[72] Jesus is taunted, as was the psalmist,

---

68. Matthew 22:41–45.

69. See chapter 6, below.

70. Psalm 41:9; Matthew 26:23. Note that Judas, who betrayed Jesus, later hangs himself (Matthew 27:5), as did Ahithophel, David's betrayer (2 Samuel 17:23).

71. Psalm 69:21; Matthew 27:34 (verse 48 also echoes the psalm).

72. Psalm 22:18; Matthew 27:35.

that the God in whom he trusts is nowhere to be found.[73] Jesus cries out to God in his abandonment, using a direct quotation from the psalms.[74]

It is thus not only in his rule that the Messiah surpasses the greatness of his forefather David; greater, too, were his sufferings.

The Babylonian Exile

Six centuries before the birth of Jesus, Nebuchadnezzar and his Babylonian forces captured Jerusalem, destroyed its temple, replaced its king (a descendant of David) with a governor of Nebuchadnezzar's own appointment, and took many Jews into exile in Babylon.[75] Inevitably the events figured largely in Israel's dialogue with the Almighty.

> Not only in his rule does the Messiah surpass the greatness of his forefather David; greater, too, were his sufferings.

Some Jews, indeed, took what had happened as a signal to worship deities they deemed more competent than the Lord.[76] Others believed that the Lord had abandoned or forgotten them.[77] Still others at least wondered what the Lord was up to and whether it was not high time, for his own sake as well as his people's, that God reaffirm his commitment to Israel.[78] On the other hand, even before Jerusalem fell, prophets such as Ezekiel in Babylon and Jeremiah in Jerusalem declared that the Lord was fighting *against* his people; Jerusalem was doomed, they said,

---

73. Psalm 22:8; Matthew 27:43.

74. Psalm 22:1; Matthew 27:46.

75. This occurred in 586 BCE. The city had already fallen to Nebuchadnezzar in 597, and a number of Jews (including the prophet Ezekiel) were then taken into exile. But 586, when Solomon's temple was destroyed and the Davidic monarchy ended, marked the greater turning point in Israel's history. (Note that after the reign of David's son Solomon, the Israelite kingdom had split into two kingdoms: Israel in the north, and Judah in the south. Judah, whose capital was Jerusalem, alone retained a Davidic monarch. The northern kingdom fell to the Assyrians in 722 BCE; it was Judah that later fell to the Babylonians.)

76. See Jeremiah 44:15–19.

77. Isaiah 40:27. Note also the accusations that Isaiah 50:1 is designed to answer.

78. See Psalms 74 and 79; note also Lamentations 5:19–22.

not because of Babylonian strength but because the Lord was pouring out his wrath on his people's sins.[79]

Still, Jerusalem was the city of God,[80] its inhabitants the Lord's covenant people. However unfaithful Israel had been, a covenant initiated by God could never end in failure. The poet who wrote the biblical book of Lamentations was as convinced as any that God's own hand had destroyed Jerusalem.

> The Lord has destroyed without mercy
>   all the dwellings of Jacob;
> in his wrath he has broken down
>   the strongholds of daughter Judah;
> he has brought down to the ground in dishonor
>   the kingdom and its rulers.
> He has cut down in fierce anger
>   all the might of Israel;
> he has withdrawn his right hand from them
>   in the face of the enemy;
> he has burned like a flaming fire in Jacob,
>   consuming all around.
> He has bent his bow like an enemy,
>   with his right hand set like a foe;
> he has killed all in whom we took pride
>   in the tent of daughter Zion;
> he has poured out his fury like fire.
> The Lord has become like an enemy;
>   he has destroyed Israel.
> He has destroyed all its palaces,
>   laid in ruins its strongholds,
> and multiplied in daughter Judah
>   mourning and lamentation.[81]

Yet precisely because the destruction came from Israel's God, hope remained that God would restore her.

> But this I call to mind,
>   and therefore I have hope:
> The steadfast love of the LORD never ceases,
>   his mercies never come to an end;

79. Jeremiah 21:3–10; 25:1–11; Ezekiel 5:5–17; 12:1–15, and elsewhere.
80. Psalm 48:1.
81. Lamentations 2:2–5.

they are new every morning;
     great is your faithfulness. . . .
It is good for one to bear
     the yoke in youth,
to sit alone in silence
     when the Lord has imposed it,
to put one's mouth to the dust
     (there may yet be hope),
to give one's cheek to the smiter,
     and be filled with insults.
For the Lord will not reject forever.
Although he causes grief, he will have compassion
     according to the abundance of his steadfast love;
for he does not willingly afflict
     or grieve anyone.[82]

The same line of thought is expressed by the prophets who
foretold Jerusalem's destruction. Using a variety of pictures
(the point did not lie in the details), they told of a glorious
future for God's people, restored, beyond judgment, to their
homeland.

I [God] have loved you with an everlasting love;
     therefore I have continued my faithfulness to you.
Again I will build you, and you shall be built,
     O virgin Israel!
Again you shall take your tambourines,
     and go forth in the dance of the merrymakers.
Again you shall plant vineyards
     on the mountains of Samaria;
the planters shall plant,
     and shall enjoy the fruit.
For there shall be a day when sentinels will call
     in the hill country of Ephraim:
"Come, let us go up to Zion,
     to the Lord our God."[83]

When the Persians overthrew the Babylonian Empire and
Cyrus, the Persian king, allowed exiled Jews to return to their

82. Lamentations 3:21–33.
83. Jeremiah 31:3–6; see all of Jeremiah 31–33; also Ezekiel 36–37, 40–48; Isaiah
40–55.

homeland,[84] Jews saw God at work, keeping his promises and showing favor once again to his people.[85] As time passed, however, it became clear that God's promises had been fulfilled only in part. Jews were back in the land they were promised; but their return had been something other than a triumphal procession,[86] and the harvests they now encountered were not plentiful.[87] The rebuilt temple was a far cry from that of Ezekiel's vision,[88] and the wealth and worship of other nations were not finding their way to Jerusalem as prophets said they would.[89] Jerusalem's enemies were not weaponless,[90] and walls of defense were still needed around the city.[91] After the exile, we may say, life returned to normal in Judah.

So *we* may say; but faithful Jews could not.[92] Those who believe in the goodness of God can explain the presence of evil in God's creation, but they can never accept it as normal. Injustice and deprivation, on the one hand, and human ignorance and defiance of God, on the other, can only be temporary. Someday God must be seen to be God by all his creatures. Someday God's own commitment to all that is good and right must be reflected on the earth God created. And someday God's love for his covenant people, reciprocated by their faithful obedience, must bring about their prosperity and peace.

> But the earth will be filled
> with the knowledge of the glory of the LORD,
> as the waters cover the sea.[93]

> Those who believe in the goodness of God can explain the presence of evil in God's creation, but they can never accept it as normal. Injustice and deprivation, on the one hand, and human ignorance and defiance of God, on the other, can only be temporary. Someday God must be seen to be God by all his creation.

84. In 539 BCE.
85. See Ezra 1:1–4 and, presumably, Psalm 126.
86. Note Ezra 8:21–23; contrast Isaiah 48:20–21; 49:8–12, 22–23; 51:11.
87. Nehemiah 5:1–3; Haggai 1:6.
88. Ezra 3:12–13; Haggai 2:1–3; contrast Ezekiel 40:1–43:12.
89. Contrast Isaiah 45:14; 55:5; 60:5–7; Haggai 2:6–9.
90. Contrast Isaiah 54:17.
91. Nehemiah 2:13–17; contrast Zechariah 2:4–5.
92. See the poignant words of Isaiah 62:1, 6–12.
93. Habakkuk 2:14.

> Say among the nations, "The LORD is king!
>> The world is firmly established; it shall never be moved.
>> He will judge the peoples with equity."
> Let the heavens be glad, and let the earth rejoice;
>> let the sea roar, and all that fills it;
>> let the field exult, and everything in it.
> Then shall all the trees of the forest sing for joy
>> before the LORD; for he is coming,
>> for he is coming to judge the earth.
> He will judge the world with righteousness,
>> and the peoples with his truth.[94]

> The days are surely coming, says the Lord, when I will raise up for David a righteous Branch, and he shall reign as king and deal wisely, and shall execute justice and righteousness in the land. In his days Judah will be saved and Israel will live in safety. And this is the name by which he will be called: "The Lord is our righteousness."[95]

No one believed that those days had come while Herod the Great ruled in Jerusalem. Yet among faithful Jews in many circles, hope remained fervent.

According to Matthew, Jesus came to fulfill the law and the prophets.[96] Matthew means more than that particular prophecies came true in the course of Jesus' life (though he is certainly convinced that they did).[97] The point is rather that all Israel's history—from Abraham through Moses, David, and the Babylonian exile—is summed up and reaches its climax in the life and proclamation of Jesus. The moment for which the faithful have waited has arrived.

Something greater than the temple is here.[98]

Something greater than Jonah is here![99]

Something greater than Solomon is here![100]

94. Psalm 96:10–13.
95. Jeremiah 23:5–6.
96. Matthew 5:17.
97. Matthew 1:22–23; 2:3–6, 15, 17–18, 23, and elsewhere.
98. Matthew 12:6.
99. Matthew 12:41.
100. Matthew 12:42.

Blessed are your eyes, for they see, and your ears, for they hear. Truly I tell you, many prophets and righteous people longed to see what you see, but did not see it, and to hear what you hear, but did not hear it.[101]

With Jesus, the reign of God is dawning.[102] To this announcement we must now turn.

---

101. Matthew 13:16–17. Note also the implications of identifying Jesus with "the one who is to come" (11:3).
102. Matthew 4:17; 10:7.

5

Dawn of a New Age

From that time Jesus began to proclaim, "Repent, for the kingdom of heaven has come near."[1]

W ith these words Matthew both begins the story of Jesus' public career and sums up the substance of Jesus' message. The message is the same when Jesus later sends out his disciples, extending the outreach of his mission: "As you go, proclaim the good news, 'The kingdom of heaven has come near.'"[2]

For Matthew and other writers of the Bible, the kingdom (or reign) of God is eternal: God would not *be* God if he were not always in control.[3] No conviction was more basic to their way of thinking than this, and none more deeply felt; yet they, too, were

1. Matthew 4:17.
2. Matthew 10:7.
3. See, for example, Psalm 103:19; 145:11–13; Daniel 4:3, 34–35. Matthew occasionally uses the expression "kingdom of God" (Matthew 12:28; 19:24; 21:31, 43; the phrase is used consistently in Mark and Luke) but generally prefers "kingdom of heaven." In Jewish circles "heaven" was commonly substituted for "God" as a sign of

constantly confronted by the reality that bad things happen in God's world. If God really is in control of the world as we know it, and as they knew it, then either God himself is not good or God allows beings who are not good a great deal of scope for their activities. The latter alternative, for Matthew and his colleagues, must be the true one: if God created beings with minds of their own (and God did), then God must surely have been prepared for the possibility that they would go their own way (and they have). In the end, however, God's goodness must assert itself. The existence of evil and human ignorance and defiance of God can all be explained. But they remain aberrations, at odds with the goodness that underlies our lives and all God's creation; and aberrations cannot be sustained forever. God's rule will one day be acknowledged by all God's creatures and reflected in the justice, righteousness, peace, and prosperity that prevail among them. In *this* sense, the kingdom of God is to be expected in the future. When it comes, God's name will be given due reverence in all the world, and his will will be done on earth as it now is in heaven.[4]

To say, then, that "the kingdom of heaven has come near" is to say that God is about to put things right and establish his righteous rule on earth. This chapter will consider how, in Matthew's Gospel, Jesus inaugurates the reign of God.

The Invitation to God's Kingdom

As God's rule embraces all his creatures, so the invitation to participate in the life of the new age is extended to all. In the first place, and in keeping with the agenda set forth in God's covenant with Abraham,[5] the message is brought to Israel. But before the end can come, the "good news of the kingdom" must be "proclaimed throughout the world"[6] so that people from east and west alike may banquet with Abraham, Isaac, and Jacob in the kingdom of heaven.[7]

---

reverence for the deity (see, for example, Matthew 21:25; Luke 15:18, 21). The phrases are equivalent in meaning.

4. So Matthew 6:9–10.
5. See chapter 4, above.
6. Matthew 24:14; see also 28:19–20.
7. Matthew 8:11.

No one is to be excluded who desires to be there. Past sins are no problem, provided people are willing to leave their past behind and come. All, to be sure, need God's forgiveness if they are to live in God's kingdom; yet God is willing—indeed, anxious—to forgive the sins of any who will come to his banquet.[8] Divine magnanimity is reflected in Jesus' life as well as his preaching: he welcomes into his company society's most notorious "sinners"—tax collectors and prostitutes—disregarding the carping of those who take offense.

> No one is to be excluded from God's kingdom who desires to be there. Past sins are no problem, provided people are willing to leave their past behind and come.

> And as [Jesus] sat at dinner in the house, many tax collectors and sinners came and were sitting with him and his disciples. When the Pharisees saw this, they said to his disciples, "Why does your teacher eat with tax collectors and sinners?" But when he heard this, he said, "Those who are well have no need of a physician, but those who are sick. Go and learn what this means, 'I desire mercy, not sacrifice.' For I have come to call not the righteous but sinners."[9]

The offer is extended to all—but it is an *offer*; the God who made people with minds of their own forces his kingdom on none. Who, one might wonder, would turn down an invitation to share the joys of God's eternal kingdom? But decide one must.

> The invitation to God's kingdom is extended to all—but it is an *offer*. The God who made people with minds of their own forces his kingdom on none.

> The kingdom of heaven is like treasure hidden in a field, which someone found and hid; then in his joy he goes and sells all that he has and buys that field. Again, the kingdom of heaven is like a merchant in search of fine pearls; on finding one pearl of great value, he went and sold all that he had and bought it.[10]

Experience soon showed, however, that many were not interested. Another parable of Jesus signals both the universality of

---

8. That much evil resides in the human heart is assumed throughout Matthew's Gospel; see Matthew 7:11; 15:18–19. The wrongs we experience at the hands of other human beings are trivial in comparison with the sins that God must forgive us all (see Matthew 18:21–35).

9. Matthew 9:10–13.

10. Matthew 13:44–46.

the invitation to God's kingdom and the casualness with which it is commonly dismissed.

> The kingdom of heaven may be compared to a king who gave a wedding banquet for his son. He sent his slaves to call those who had been invited to the wedding banquet, but they would not come. Again he sent other slaves, saying, "Tell those who have been invited: Look, I have prepared my dinner; my oxen and my fat calves have been slaughtered, and everything is ready; come to the wedding banquet." But they made light of it and went away, one to his farm, another to his business, while the rest seized his slaves, mistreated them, and killed them. The king was enraged. He sent his troops, destroyed those murderers, and burned their city.[11] Then he said to his slaves, "The wedding is ready, but those invited were not worthy. Go therefore into the main streets, and invite everyone you find to the wedding banquet." Those slaves went out into the streets and gathered all whom they found, both good and bad; so the wedding hall was filled with guests.[12]

In yet another parable, Jesus compares those who hear the message of the kingdom to the ground on which a farmer tosses his seed.[13] Some soil proves too hard for seed to penetrate. Other soil is rocky and does not allow the seed to take root. Still elsewhere grain that begins to grow is choked by thorns and dies. Only a portion of the seed falls on fertile soil and brings a good harvest. In the same way, Jesus' message of the kingdom is heard by all kinds of people and meets with all kinds of responses; but those who take it to heart are few.[14]

What, in practice, did it mean to accept Jesus' message of the kingdom? And why, in Matthew's view, did many decline the offer?

---

11. The parable within the parable—recipients of the message bring on their own destruction by mistreating the king's messengers—reflects the conviction that the fall of Jerusalem (70 CE) was a divine punishment for its abuse of God's messengers (and, in particular, God's Son). See the discussion in chapter 4 (under the heading "Abraham"), above.

12. Matthew 22:2–10.

13. Matthew 13:3–9, 18–23.

14. Note that in Jesus' explanation of the parable, all four groups are said to "hear" the "word of the kingdom" (Matthew 13:19, 20, 22, 23), but only the fourth group "understands" it (that is, grasps it and takes it to heart). The concluding admonition ("Let anyone with ears listen" [13:9]) stresses the responsibility of all who hear Jesus' message to take it to heart.

1. For some, to accept the invitation meant, quite literally, to leave what they were doing and join the band of Jesus' followers.

As [Jesus] walked by the Sea of Galilee, he saw two brothers, Simon, who is called Peter, and Andrew his brother, casting a net into the sea—for they were fishermen. And he said to them, "Follow me, and I will make you fish for people." Immediately they left their nets and followed him. As he went from there, he saw two other brothers, James son of Zebedee and his brother John, in the boat with their father Zebedee, mending their nets, and he called them. Immediately they left the boat and their father, and followed him.[15]

> Jesus' message of the kingdom is heard by all kinds of people and meets with all kinds of responses; but those who take it to heart are few.

As Jesus was walking along, he saw a man called Matthew sitting at the tax booth; and he said to him, "Follow me." And he got up and followed him.[16]

Not all were called to follow Jesus physically; but all must adopt a lifestyle in keeping with God's goodness, as Jesus demanded.

Come to me, all you that are weary and are carrying heavy burdens, and I will give you rest. Take my yoke upon you, and learn from me; for I am gentle and humble in heart, and you will find rest for your souls. For my yoke is easy, and my burden is light.[17]

We have already seen in part what this entails:[18] serving God rather than wealth, and trusting God to supply one's needs; renouncing insults as well as murder, lust as well as adultery, the unfaithfulness that seeks to escape from marriage commitments as well as that which flagrantly violates them, oaths and all untruthfulness, retribution and "sticking up for one's rights," and every restriction on the scope of one's love. Such is life as guided by God's goodness, life that cannot but emerge as light in the world's darkness and bring glory to God.[19] God is, moreover,

15. Matthew 4:18–22.
16. Matthew 9:9.
17. Matthew 11:28–30.
18. See chapters 2 and 3, above. The life of discipleship will be discussed in more detail in chapter 7, below.
19. Matthew 5:16.

infinitely forgiving of the failures of his children. But only those who love God, trust God, and hunger for his goodness know God as their Father. Only those out of step with the values of this age will have a part in the age to come.

> Blessed are the poor in spirit, for theirs is the kingdom of heaven.
> Blessed are those who mourn, for they will be comforted.
> Blessed are the meek, for they will inherit the earth.
> Blessed are those who hunger and thirst for righteousness, for they will be filled.
> Blessed are the merciful, for they will receive mercy.
> Blessed are the pure in heart, for they will see God.
> Blessed are the peacemakers, for they will be called children of God.
> Blessed are those who are persecuted for righteousness' sake, for theirs is the kingdom of heaven.
> Blessed are you when people revile you and persecute you and utter all kinds of evil against you falsely on my account. Rejoice and be glad, for your reward is great in heaven, for in the same way they persecuted the prophets who were before you.[20]

Only those who love God, trust God, and hunger for his goodness know God as their Father. Only those out of step with the values of this age will have a part in the age to come.

2. If, to participate in the new age, we must adopt its goodness as our lifestyle, those who have invested in the values of the present age may well be unable, or lack the interest, to take up the offer. In Jesus' parable of the wedding banquet, the king's invitation is turned down by those who prefer to get on with their farm or business.[21] In the parable of the farmer who sows seed on different types of soil, the thorns that choke the sprouting grain are said to represent "the cares of the world and the lure of

20. Matthew 5:3–12. These "beatitudes" will be discussed briefly in chapter 7.
21. Matthew 22:5. And is the point of 8:34 ("Then the whole town came out to meet Jesus; and when they saw him, they begged him to leave their neighborhood") that Jesus was perceived as a threat to business as usual?

wealth."[22] Attachment to worldly goods proves too strong, too, for a young man otherwise eager to enter the kingdom: when told to sell his possessions, give the money to the poor, and follow Jesus, he goes away "grieving, for he had many possessions."[23] Jesus responds in sobering terms: "It is easier for a camel to go through the eye of a needle than for someone who is rich to enter the kingdom of God."[24]

By no means are those who decline a place in God's kingdom confined to the irreligious. To the latter, indeed, the path of repentance is always open. The religious, on the other hand, may see no need for repentance—though they live no less than others in defiance of God's will.

> If, to participate in the new age, we must adopt its goodness as our lifestyle, those who have invested in the values of the present age may well be unable, or lack the interest, to take up the offer.

[Jesus spoke:] "What do you[25] think? A man had two sons; he went to the first and said, 'Son, go and work in the vineyard today.' He answered, 'I will not'; but later he changed his mind and went. The father went to the second and said the same; and he answered, 'I go, sir'; but he did not go. Which of the two did the will of his father?" They said, "The first." Jesus said to them, "Truly I tell you, the tax collectors and the prostitutes are going into the kingdom of God ahead of you. For John came to you in the way of righteousness and you did not believe him, but the tax collectors and the prostitutes believed him; and even after you saw it, you did not change your minds and believe him."[26]

There is nothing obscure about *this* parable! When tax collectors and prostitutes chose their profession, they were, in effect, saying no to the God who forbids dishonesty, greed,[27] and immorality; but when John told them to repent, many did (thus changing their minds and, in effect, saying yes to God). On the

---

22. Matthew 13:22.

23. Matthew 19:16–22. See also 8:19–20.

24. Matthew 19:24.

25. "You" here is "the chief priests and the elders of the people" (see Matthew 21:23).

26. Matthew 21:28–32.

27. In Jesus' day, tax collectors had a well-earned reputation for dishonesty and greed.

other hand, certain religious people may have *said* yes to God when they chose to be religious; but their way of life belies their claims, and their refusal to listen to John proves that religiosity is for them a shield against the demands of God rather than a renunciation of self-seeking.[28] Predictably, then, they turn a deaf ear when Jesus invites them to God's kingdom.

> Religious people may see no need for repentance—even though they live no less than others in defiance of God's will.

Even better disguised but no less real is the rejection of Jesus' invitation shown by those who greet his words with enthusiasm, join the circle of his followers, but fail to put his teaching into practice. Sinners they were when they were welcomed into his company; but they cannot continue to live in sin if they would one day be reckoned with the righteous.[29] Nor is holy bustle in Jesus' name a substitute for obeying God.

> Not everyone who says to me, "Lord, Lord," will enter the kingdom of heaven, but only the one who does the will of my Father in heaven. On that day many will say to me, "Lord, Lord, did we not prophesy in your name, and cast out demons in your name, and do many deeds of power in your name?" Then I will declare to them, "I never knew you; go away from me, you evildoers."[30]

Even would-be followers of Jesus must forgive those who wrong them if they would not be ranked with the unforgiven.[31]

> No less real is the rejection of Jesus' invitation shown by those who greet his words with enthusiasm, join the circle of his followers, but fail to put his teaching into practice.

And if they do not treat Jesus with kindness when they meet him in the person of their needy neighbor, they will find themselves one day banished from his presence.

> Then [the king] will say to those at his left hand, "You that are accursed, depart from me into the eternal fire

28. For the notion that adherence to religious traditions may shield practitioners from the true demands of God, see Matthew 15:3–9; 23:23–24. For the self-seeking of people who are outwardly religious, see Matthew 6:1–6, 16–18; 23:5–12, 25–28.

29. This seems to be the point of Matthew 22:11–13; see also 5:20; 24:45–51.

30. Matthew 7:21–23.

31. Matthew 6:14–15; 18:21–35.

prepared for the devil and his angels; for I was hungry and you gave me no food, I was thirsty and you gave me nothing to drink, I was a stranger and you did not welcome me, naked and you did not give me clothing, sick and in prison and you did not visit me." Then they also will answer, "Lord, when was it that we saw you hungry or thirsty or a stranger or naked or sick or in prison, and did not take care of you?" Then he will answer them, "Truly I tell you, just as you did not do it to one of the least of these, you did not do it to me." And these will go away into eternal punishment, but the righteous into eternal life.[32]

From the very gates of heaven, Matthew warns us, there is a way to hell.

Finally we should note that the rejection of Jesus' message cannot be dissociated from rejection of the messenger. The kingdom of God is offered in the message of Jesus, and those who "hunger and thirst" for God and his "righteousness" find joy in receiving it.[33] In Jesus' words, they already

> While people with faith see in this tiniest of seeds the promise of God's kingdom, others are "put off" by its unpretentious appearance.

"have" a heart that is open and willing to receive God's kingdom, and "more" understanding is given to them.[34] But the principle remains true: God's kingdom is not forced upon anyone. Its presence is not announced with a supernatural display for all to see—a display that would, in effect, leave them no choice but to believe;[35] rather it is veiled in the very human appearance of Jesus. Those, then, who do not "have" a deep hunger for God see nothing more than a carpenter's son from Nazareth whose family they know,[36] surrounded by local fishermen, a tax collector, and others anonymous in all but name.[37] Thus, while those with faith see in this tiniest of seeds the promise of God's kingdom,[38] others are "put

32. Matthew 25:41–46.

33. Matthew 5:6; see also 6:33; 13:44–46.

34. Matthew 13:12.

35. As we will see in the next section, the Jesus of Matthew's Gospel performs many miracles but with as little show as possible (see, for example, Matthew 8:4; 9:30; 12:15–19) and only in response to need; requests for miraculous proofs are consistently denied. Those disinclined to believe are quick to find other explanations for Jesus' miracles than the presence of God's power (Matthew 9:34; 12:24).

36. Matthew 13:54–58.

37. Matthew 10:2–4.

38. Matthew 13:31–32.

off"—"offended" is the standard English translation—by the unexpectedly low key in which the kingdom theme is introduced. Jesus observes, "Blessed is anyone who takes no offense at me [= who is not put off by the unpretentiousness of my appearance]."[39]

The Power of God's Kingdom

If the world as we know it is subject to God's rule, then God must allow beings who are not good considerable scope for their activities. Those who refuse to live in harmony with creation's moral order, preferring to pursue their self-interest, quickly find themselves part of a world marred by conflict, exploitation, and acts of violence: such is life on our earth. Nothing of this reflects God's goodness, nor will God allow the perversion and ruin of his creation to continue forever. Moreover, sickness, disease, demonic oppression,[40] and death are also signs of creation's present disorder: no more than violence and the corruption of justice are they to be accepted as the normal stuff of human life. They, too, will be done away with when God reasserts his rule.

39. Matthew 11:6.
40. For Matthew, as for Jesus, God's rebellious creatures include demonic powers as well as the people whom they tempt and oppress. Note the reference to Satan's "kingdom" in 12:26. See also 5:37; 6:13; 13:38; 25:41.

Dietrich Bonhoeffer did not hesitate to say that demons ruled the world in August 1932:

> Events are coming to a head more terribly than ever before—*millions hungry,* men with cruelly deferred and unfulfilled wishes, desperate men who have nothing to lose but their lives and will lose nothing in losing them—humiliated and degraded nations who cannot get over their shame—*political extreme against political extreme, fanatic against fanatic,* idol against idol, and behind it all a world which bristles with weapons as never before, a world which feverishly arms to guarantee peace through arming . . . —how can one close one's eyes at the fact that the demons themselves have taken over the rule of the world, that it is the powers of darkness who have here made an awful conspiracy and could break out at any moment?—how could one think that these demons could be driven out, these powers annihilated with a bit of education in international understanding, with a bit of good will? Would it not be blasphemous frivolity to think that the devil could be exorcised with the cry "No more War" and with a new organization—even if it be a Christian organization? . . . Our good intentions, our talk of peace and good will is nothing, unless the Lord himself comes and drives out the demons. (*No Rusty Swords: Letters, Lectures, and Notes, 1928–1936* [London: Collins, 1970], 182–83)

Matthew's Jesus does more than announce God's coming kingdom and invite all to its table. The power of God that will one day banish disease, oppression, and death is already at work in Jesus' activities, healing the sick, setting free the oppressed, raising the dead. In deeds as well as words, Jesus announces the dawn of God's kingdom.

Then they brought to him a demoniac who was blind and mute; and he cured him, so that the one who had been mute could speak and see. All the crowds were amazed and said, "Can this be the Son of David?" But when the Pharisees heard it, they said, "It is only by Beelzebul, the ruler of the demons, that this fellow casts out the demons." He knew what they were thinking and said to them, "Every kingdom divided against itself is laid waste, and no city or house divided against itself will stand. If Satan casts out Satan, he is divided against himself; how then will his kingdom stand? . . . But if it is by the Spirit of God that I cast out demons, then the kingdom of God has come to you."[41]

Such accounts strike many today as coming from a different age, an age that had a place (as our own, for many, does not) for intrusions into the natural world by the supernatural. Certainly Matthew's worldview is different; yet it is essential to his story that the powers of Jesus are without precedent or parallel even in the eyes of people prepared to accept the miraculous.[42] The God whose patience has long been tried by the corruption of his creation is now beginning to put things right.

> The power of God that will one day banish disease, oppression, and death is already at work in Jesus' activities.

When John heard in prison what the Messiah was doing, he sent word by his disciples and said to him, "Are you the one who is to come, or are we to wait for another?" Jesus answered them, "Go and tell John what you hear and see: the blind receive their sight, the lame walk, the lepers are cleansed, the deaf hear, the dead are raised, and the poor have good news brought to them. And blessed is anyone who takes no offense at me."[43]

41. Matthew 12:22–28.
42. Matthew 9:33.
43. Matthew 11:2–6.

As Jesus extends
the invitation
to the kingdom
to all who will
enter, so he makes
available its
power to all who
seek it in faith.

Jesus' acts of healing are, of course, acts of compassion as well as manifestations of the power of God's kingdom.[44] As Jesus extends the invitation to the kingdom to all who will enter, so he makes available its power to all who seek it in faith.

When Jesus had come down from the mountain, great crowds followed him; and there was a leper who came to him and knelt before him, saying, "Lord, if you choose, you can make me clean." He stretched out his hand and touched him, saying, "I do choose. Be made clean!" Immediately his leprosy was cleansed.[45]

Suddenly a woman who had been suffering from hemorrhages for twelve years came up behind him and touched the fringe of his cloak, for she said to herself, "If I only touch his cloak, I will be made well." Jesus turned, and seeing her he said, "Take heart, daughter; your faith has made you well." And instantly the woman was made well.[46]

As Jesus went on from there, two blind men followed him, crying loudly, "Have mercy on us, Son of David!" When he entered the house, the blind men came to him; and Jesus said to them, "Do you believe that I am able to do this?" They said to him, "Yes, Lord." Then he touched their eyes and said, "According to your faith let it be done to you." And their eyes were opened.[47]

Still, not all requests are granted. When God's help is sincerely sought, Jesus gives it; when proof of God's presence and power is demanded, Jesus refuses.[48] The faith of those who turn to God as their only source of aid is always rewarded by divine interventions. But such interventions can never create true faith in those disinclined to believe, and Jesus does not tolerate the insolence of those who insist that before they will acknowledge the presence of God, God must satisfy their terms.

Then [Jesus] began to reproach the cities in which most of his deeds of power had been done, because they did not repent. "Woe to you,

44. Matthew 9:35–36; 14:14; 20:34.
45. Matthew 8:1–3.
46. Matthew 9:20–22.
47. Matthew 9:27–30.
48. Contrast Matthew 24:24.

Chorazin! Woe to you, Bethsaida! For if the deeds of power done in you had been done in Tyre and Sidon, they would have repented long ago in sackcloth and ashes. But I tell you, on the day of judgment it will be more tolerable for Tyre and Sidon than for you. And you, Capernaum,

> will you be exalted to heaven?

> No, you will be brought down to Hades.

For if the deeds of power done in you had been done in Sodom, it would have remained until this day. But I tell you that on the day of judgment it will be more tolerable for the land of Sodom than for you."[49]

The Pharisees and Sadducees came, and to test Jesus they asked him to show them a sign from heaven. He answered them, "When it is evening, you say, 'It will be fair weather, for the sky is red.' And in the morning, 'It will be stormy today, for the sky is red and threatening.' You know how to interpret the appearance of the sky, but you cannot interpret the signs of the times. An evil and adulterous generation asks for a sign, but no sign will be given to it except the sign of Jonah."[50] Then he left them and went away.[51]

The Course of God's Kingdom

The seed that will grow into God's kingdom is already now being planted.[52] The power of God's kingdom to heal and restore is already at work. The summons to prepare for the kingdom is being published throughout Israel. A new age is dawning. But it will not come fully until Jesus himself returns to earth, in power and glory, as the judge of humankind.[53] All are now invited to the kingdom; but if the new age of goodness is not quickly to revert to the corruption of the old, only those willing to side with the

---

49. Matthew 11:20–24.

50. See Matthew 12:38–41.

51. Matthew 16:1–4. Along similar lines, Jesus refuses to answer those who demand to know the source of his authority. That those who put the question are triflers not in honest pursuit of the truth was already apparent in their unwillingness to listen to John the Baptist. It is confirmed by their refusal to consider seriously Jesus' question about the source of John's authority; their concern is rather to score points or save face in a debate (Matthew 21:23–27).

52. Matthew 13:31–32.

53. Matthew 13:41–43; 16:27; 24:30–31; 25:31–46.

good can gain entrance. Those who now refuse God's rule can have no share in its coming glory.

In the meantime, the good news of the kingdom must continue to be spread, among Jews in the first place, but after Jesus' departure among Gentiles as well.

> And this good news of the kingdom will be proclaimed throughout the world, as a testimony to all the nations; and then the end will come.[54]

A new age is dawning. But it will not come fully until Jesus himself returns to earth, in power and glory, as the judge of humankind.

By their response to the messengers of the kingdom, people determine their destiny.[55] Many will be hostile. Messengers of the kingdom are sent out "like sheep into the midst of wolves."[56] They will be maligned, abused, put on trial, perhaps put to death, always hated: such is the lot of the good in a world more tolerant of evil.[57] Jesus' followers are to expect opposition, to fear none but God, and to be reassured that those who endure to the end will be saved.[58] Some, indeed, will fall away, put off by the hardships; others, losing their fervor as the Lord seems to delay his return, will grow slack or revert to old ways.[59] Those, however, who remain vigilant and faithful to their mission will be commended and rewarded by their Lord when he returns.[60]

The old age will not go away without a struggle. As the end draws near, lawlessness and wars will increase, false prophets will proliferate, disasters will follow hard on disasters.[61] The faithful are not to be shaken or misled: their Lord will indeed return, and there will be no mistaking his reappearance.[62]

When will all this take place? In Matthew's Gospel, it already *is* taking place: as the dawn of the kingdom has come, so opposition

---

54. Matthew 24:14.
55. Matthew 10:14–15, 40–42.
56. Matthew 10:16.
57. Note what Matthew says about the typical fate of prophets (Matthew 5:12; 23:29–35) and what he records about the fate of John the Baptist (14:1–12; 17:11–13).
58. Matthew 10:16–31.
59. Matthew 13:21; 24:45–25:13.
60. Matthew 25:14–23.
61. Matthew 24:4–29.
62. Matthew 24:30–31.

to the kingdom has begun.[63] Already messengers of the kingdom encounter hostility. On the other hand, Jesus must depart from the scene before he can return to it in glory;[64] his absence must be sufficiently extended to test the faithfulness of his followers; the good news of the kingdom has to be brought to all the world, and times of great trouble must transpire before the end will come. Moreover, the "day and hour" of the end are known only to the Father: not to the angels, not even to Jesus (God's "Son"), and still less to Jesus' followers, whose diligence and vigilance are put to the test precisely by their ignorance on this score.[65] Nonetheless, the end cannot be far off.

> Jesus' followers are to expect opposition, to fear none but God, and to be reassured that those who endure to the end will be saved.

> Truly I tell you, there are some standing here who will not taste death before they see the Son of Man coming in his kingdom.[66]

> Truly I tell you, this generation[67] will not pass away until all these things have taken place.[68]

Is the message of the Gospel, then, that Jesus will return before all his contemporaries have "tasted death"? This is clearly the most natural reading of the texts just cited, and it fits well with the common early Christian conviction that the end was near.[69] On the other hand, the events listed as required to take place before the end comes are not few, and the Gospel concludes with a monumental commission and a promise, both of which imply a protracted period of time prior to history's consummation:

63. This seems to be the point of Jesus' obscure words in Matthew 11:12: "From the days of John the Baptist until now the kingdom of heaven has suffered violence, and the violent take it by force."

64. Note Matthew 9:15; 25:14–19.

65. Matthew 24:36–25:13.

66. Matthew 16:28.

67. It is sometimes suggested that the Greek word *genea* here refers to Israel as a nation or to a particular category of people. But the parallel with 16:28 and Matthew's usage of the term elsewhere (see, for example, Matthew 11:16; 12:41–42) favor the rendering "generation."

68. Matthew 24:34.

69. See, for example, Romans 13:11–12; 1 Corinthians 7:29–31; 1 Peter 4:7; 1 John 2:18; Revelation 1:1; 22:7, 10, 12, 20.

Go therefore and make disciples of all nations, baptizing them in the name of the Father and of the Son and of the Holy Spirit, and teaching them to obey everything that I have commanded you. And remember, I am with you always, to the end of the age.[70]

Perhaps we ought simply to respect the integrity of both types of text and leave the issue unresolved. Alternatively, we might perhaps see as the point of the Gospel that the words of Jesus—like those of the prophets who forecast a glorious future for Israel after the exile[71]—have found sufficient fulfillment in subsequent events to confirm their truthfulness, though aspects of what he (and they) called for remain to be realized.[72] Three of Jesus' disciples *did* catch a glimpse of his glory when, on a "high mountain, . . . he was transfigured before them."[73] God's rule *did* reach a new stage when the resurrected Jesus was given "all authority in heaven and on earth."[74] Divine judgment on those who rejected the messengers of the kingdom *did* fall on Jerusalem when the Romans destroyed it.[75] Jesus' words, in short, had by no means fallen to the ground, but had already found a measure of fulfillment in history. It was, moreover, certain that in God's good time[76] and when opportunities for humans to repent[77] had

70. Matthew 28:19–20. See also 24:14, 48; 25:5, 19.

71. See the discussion in chapter 4, above, under the heading "The Babylonian Exile."

72. Something along these lines is perhaps suggested already by the lack of anxiety shown about the truth of Matthew 16:28 and 24:34 in a Gospel written when any straightforward fulfillment must have seemed very much in doubt. Matthew was composed, in the view of most scholars, more than half a century after the time of Jesus; surviving contemporaries of Jesus must by that time have been few, their hold on life tenuous.

73. Matthew 17:1–2.

74. Matthew 28:18.

75. See Matthew 22:7.

76. Divine freedom to adjust the outworking of divine pronouncements is affirmed by Jeremiah (18:1–11; see also 1 Samuel 2:30) and illustrated both by the story of Jonah (3:1–4:11) and by prophetic revisions of the promise of a lasting dynasty to David (see the discussion under "David" in chapter 4); it may well be assumed in Matthew's Gospel (note the flexibility assumed in Matthew 24:22; also in Luke 13:6–9). See also the following note.

77. In early Christian understanding, God's intention for the period prior to Jesus' return was to allow people time to repent and believe (see Acts 3:19–21; 2 Corinthians 6:1–2); the same consideration explained the apparent delay of that return (see 2 Peter 3:9; also Luke 13:6–9).

been exhausted, Jesus would return as he said and establish God's rule. The presence of evil in God's creation can be explained, but it can only be temporary. Sooner or later—Matthew, together with all biblical tradition, affirms—God's goodness *must* prevail.

The Cross and the Kingdom

In Matthew's Gospel, the one who inaugurates the reign of God is killed on a Roman cross. Over his head, mocking and supposedly ending his pretensions, is the very title given him in worship at the Gospel's beginning: "This is Jesus, the King of the Jews."[78]

For Matthew, Jesus' death (1) brings to a climax the hostility that God's kingdom encounters in the world; and it represents both (2) the supreme test of Jesus' own faithfulness to God's rule and (3) an indispensable stage in the coming of the kingdom.

> The presence of evil in God's creation can be explained, but it can only be temporary. Sooner or later— Matthew, together with all biblical tradition, affirms—God's goodness *must* prevail.

1. God's reign—by definition, we may say— is eternal. Human beings—by definition, we may almost say—oppose this reign. God reasserts his rule and reclaims his creatures. Such, in brief, is the story of the Bible.

The very first human beings, according to Genesis, opt for what seems good to them rather than trust the goodness of God's command: they disobey God by eating fruit from the "tree of the knowledge of good and evil."[79] This Genesis story sums up, even as it launches, the biblical story of human opposition to God: human beings are seen typically to ignore where they do not flout God's demands. In one oft-used phrase, people embrace "what is right in their own eyes," though its pursuit inevitably brings them into conflict with other human beings similarly preoccupied with self-interest. In the biblical narrative, God's covenant with Israel provides yet another forum for humanity's inclination toward evil, though now with at least two added dimensions. God gave Israel laws to

---

78. Matthew 27:37; compare 2:2.
79. Genesis 3:1–6.

remind of human responsibility and to restrain human evil, and God sent his people prophets to warn them of the consequences of their willfulness. Yet in the time of Jesus, Jews looking back on their past could regard it as a long history of disobedience to God's laws and opposition to his prophets. To this dismal assessment, Matthew would add that religious tradition proves no better an antidote to human corruption than divine laws or prophetic messengers: in the hands of wicked priests, God's temple itself had become a "den of robbers";[80] and Pharisees, though famous for their piety, are seen as more loyal to their own prescriptions than to the laws of God himself.[81]

If the story of Jesus represents the continuation and climax of God's dealings with Israel[82] and if this relationship has been marred throughout by local expressions of humanity's resistance to God's rule, then the response that greets Jesus' activities in Matthew's Gospel is predictable. People dismiss, even disdain, Jesus' invitation to participate in God's rule. Jesus' message of the coming of the kingdom and the deeds that point to its arrival are met with suspicion, slander, and outright opposition.[83] Jesus' death may seem a curious step in the establishment of God's kingdom; yet in Matthew's Gospel it represents the natural culmination—and ultimate expression—of humanity's resistance to God.[84]

> God's reign—by definition, we may say—is eternal. Human beings—by definition, we may almost say—oppose this reign.

2. Still, Jesus himself remains faithful. Matthew 4 depicts a Jesus who reenacts the experiences of Israel in the wilderness;[85] but whereas the people of Israel complained against God because of their hunger, demanded that God prove his presence in their midst at a time of crisis, and worshiped other gods, Jesus remains submissive to God and resistant to each temptation. Twice Satan presents Jesus with the opportunity to exploit his prerogatives as

---

80. Matthew 21:13, where Jesus' words echo the prophetic denunciation of Jeremiah 7:11.

81. Matthew 15:3–9, 12–13; 23:23–24.

82. For this Matthean theme, see chapter 4, above.

83. The story of Matthew's Gospel, including that of opposition to Jesus, will be traced in chapter 8, below.

84. Note how, in the parable of the wicked tenants, the abuse of the landowner's servants precedes the killing of his son (Matthew 21:33–41).

85. See the discussion under the heading "Moses" in chapter 4, above.

God's Son in ways that would compromise his obedience to the Father.[86] On both occasions Jesus refuses.

Twice in later chapters Jesus is challenged (as he was challenged by Satan) to compel God to intervene miraculously and thereby accredit Jesus. Jesus sees in each challenge the spirit of an "evil and adulterous generation" and dismisses them both.[87]

In Matthew 16, Jesus informs his disciples that "he must go to Jerusalem and undergo great suffering at the hands of the elders and chief priests and scribes, and be killed, and on the third day be raised."[88] The announcement is as distant from current expectations of the Messiah as it is abhorrent to the very human sensibilities of the disciples.

> Jesus' death may seem a curious step in the establishment of God's kingdom, yet in Matthew's Gospel it represents the natural culmination—and ultimate expression—of humanity's resistance to God.

> And Peter took him aside and began to rebuke him, saying, "God forbid it, Lord! This must never happen to you."[89]

Jesus turns on Peter with a rebuke that echoes his earlier dismissal of Satan and suggests that here, too, Jesus must resist the temptation to abandon his obedience to God.

> But [Jesus] turned and said to Peter, "Get behind me, Satan![90] You are a stumbling block to me; for you are setting your mind not on divine things but on human things."[91]

Subsequent chapters repeatedly remind us that he is journeying steadily toward Jerusalem.[92] In Jerusalem Jesus eats his last

---

86. "If you are the Son of God, command these stones to become loaves of bread" (Matthew 4:3); "If you are the Son of God, throw yourself down [from the pinnacle of the temple]; for it is written, 'He will command his angels concerning you,' and 'On their hands they will bear you up, so that you will not dash your foot against a stone'" (4:6).

87. Matthew 12:38–40; 16:1–4.

88. Matthew 16:21.

89. Matthew 16:22.

90. Compare Matthew 4:10.

91. Matthew 16:23.

92. Matthew 19:1; 20:17; 21:1, 10.

supper with his disciples, aware that he is about to be betrayed.[93] He leaves the meal with his disciples, aware that they all will soon desert him.[94] He prays alone in Gethsemane, venting his dread of the "cup" he is about to drink but submitting nonetheless to the divine purpose.

> Jesus prays alone in Gethsemane, venting his dread of the "cup" he is about to drink but submitting nonetheless to the divine purpose: "My Father, if it is possible, let this cup pass from me; yet not what I want but what you want."

My Father, if it is possible, let this cup pass from me; yet not what I want but what you want.[95]

He returns to his disciples, only to be set upon by Judas, the betrayer, and "a large crowd with swords and clubs, from the chief priests and the elders of the people."[96] Again we are reminded that the Son of God has at his disposal more than adequate resources to cope with the hostility of his foes; again he declines to depart from his Father's will.

> Suddenly, one of those with Jesus put his hand on his sword, drew it, and struck the slave of the high priest, cutting off his ear. Then Jesus said to him, "Put your sword back into its place; for all who take the sword will perish by the sword. Do you think that I cannot appeal to my Father, and he will at once send me more than twelve legions of angels? But how then would the scriptures be fulfilled, which say it must happen in this way?"[97]

In the narrative that follows, Jesus is falsely accused but remains silent;[98] spat upon, struck, and mocked but does nothing.[99] Further accusations again elicit no response;[100] flogging, stripping, continued abuse, and crucifixion itself meet no resistance.[101] Temptations that Jesus once resisted in his period of strength—the

93. Matthew 26:20–25.
94. Matthew 26:31–35.
95. Matthew 26:39.
96. Matthew 26:47.
97. Matthew 26:51–54.
98. Matthew 26:59–63.
99. Matthew 26:67–68.
100. Matthew 27:13–14.
101. Matthew 27:26–44.

temptations to exercise his prerogatives as God's Son and to compel God to intervene on his behalf and legitimate his claims—are now derisively thrown at him as he hangs on a cross.

> You who would destroy the temple and build it in three days, save yourself! If you are the Son of God, come down from the cross.

> He saved others; he cannot save himself. He is the King of Israel; let him come down from the cross now, and we will believe in him. He trusts in God; let God deliver him now, if he wants to; for he said, "I am God's Son."[102]

But Jesus refuses to use his power to "save himself." He remains on the cross, submissive to his Father's will even in his hour of death.

Matthew allows a centurion posted at Jesus' cross to remind us of the significance of what has happened: "Truly this man was God's Son!"[103] For Matthew, the supreme demonstration of Jesus' divine sonship does not lie in the miraculous powers he displayed but in his complete faithfulness to his Father's will.

> For Matthew, the supreme demonstration of Jesus' divine sonship does not lie in the miraculous powers he displayed but in his complete faithfulness to his Father's will.

3. How, then, does the death of God's Son speed the coming of the kingdom?

God's reign, though eternal in the sense that God is always in control, is in another sense yet to be established: people remain resistant to God's rule, refusing to acknowledge it or submit to God's demands; their resistance mars as it disturbs creation's order and subjects humanity to sickness, disease, demons, and death. God's power to do away with all that oppresses and his promise one day to do so are both reflected in the miracles of Jesus. But the marks of creation's disorder cannot be fully done away with while the cause of the disorder persists. Human sinfulness itself must be dealt with before God's kingdom can come.

102. Matthew 27:40, 42–43.
103. Matthew 27:54.

In the very first chapter of his Gospel, Matthew informs us that God intends, through Jesus, to bring about deliverance from sin:

> An angel of the Lord appeared to [Joseph] in a dream and said, "Joseph, son of David, do not be afraid to take Mary as your wife, for the child conceived in her is from the Holy Spirit. She will bear a son, and you are to name him Jesus, for he will save his people from their sins."[104]

When Jesus later tells his disciples that he "came not to be served but to serve, and to give his life a ransom for many,"[105] the ransom he has in mind presumably refers to the same deliverance from sin. The point becomes explicit at Jesus' last supper with his disciples. In the simple act of offering his disciples a cup from which to drink, Jesus symbolizes the giving of his life's blood for their benefit—"for the forgiveness of sins."

> Then he took a cup, and after giving thanks he gave it to them, saying, "Drink from it, all of you; for this is my blood of the covenant, which is poured out for many for the forgiveness of sins."[106]

Human sinfulness must be dealt with before God's kingdom can come.

The message of Matthew's Gospel, as of the early Christians in general, is that "Christ died for our sins."[107] Though himself faithful to God to the very end, Jesus suffered the brunt—and ultimate expression—of humanity's resistance to God when he was crucified. In his innocence he paid the price for others' misdeeds, procuring the forgiveness that opens to sinful human beings a place in God's kingdom.

104. Matthew 1:20–21. Compare Psalm 130:7–8, which similarly sees sin as that from which, ultimately, deliverance is required:
> O Israel, hope in the LORD!
> For with the LORD there is steadfast love,
>   and with him is great power to redeem.
> It is he who will redeem Israel
>   from all its iniquities.

105. Matthew 20:28.

106. Matthew 26:27–28.

107. First Corinthians 15:3. Notice how Paul sees this simple claim (together with that of Jesus' resurrection) as the substance of the gospel that he himself received and of the proclamation of all the apostles (1 Corinthians 15:1, 11).

Matthew himself tells the story without editorial comment. When early Christians sought the reason for Jesus' death, they found illumination in the words of an ancient prophet:

> Surely he has borne our infirmities
>   and carried our diseases;
> yet we accounted him stricken,
>   struck down by God, and afflicted.
> But he was wounded for our transgressions,
>   crushed for our iniquities;
> upon him was the punishment that made us whole,
>   and by his bruises we are healed.
> All we like sheep have gone astray;
>   we have all turned to our own way,
> and the LORD has laid on him
>   the iniquity of us all.[108]

> Jesus suffered the brunt—and ultimate expression—of humanity's resistance to God when he was crucified. In his innocence he paid the price for others' misdeeds, procuring the forgiveness that opens to sinful human beings a place in God's kingdom.

The Enthronement of the King

The last word in the Gospel is given not to humans who oppose God's kingdom but to God's faithful Son. Taunted on the cross for his apparent inability to save himself from death, Jesus is vindicated through the still greater triumph of overcoming death itself.[109]

After the Sabbath, as the first day of the week was dawning, Mary Magdalene and the other Mary went to see the tomb. And suddenly

---

108. Isaiah 53:4–6. Matthew's Gospel itself, in saying that Jesus "poured out" his blood *"for many* for the forgiveness of sins" (Matthew 26:28), appears to echo Isaiah 53:11–12: "The righteous one, my servant, shall make *many* righteous, and he shall bear their iniquities. . . . he bore the sin of *many*." See also Romans 4:25; Hebrews 9:28; 1 Peter 2:24–25.

109. In prison, Dietrich Bonhoeffer sent an Easter greeting to his friend Eberhard Bethge: "Easter? We're paying more attention to dying than to death. We're more concerned to get over the act of dying than to overcome death. Socrates mastered the art of dying; Christ overcame death as 'the last enemy' (1 Cor. 15.26). There is a real difference between the two things; the one is within the scope of human possibilities, the other means resurrection. It's not from *ars moriendi*, the art of dying, but from the resurrection of Christ, that a new and purifying wind can blow through our present world" (*Letters and Papers from Prison*, ed. Eberhard Bethge, expanded ed. [New York: Simon & Schuster, 1997], 240).

there was a great earthquake; for an angel of the Lord, descending from heaven, came and rolled back the stone and sat on it. His appearance was like lightning, and his clothing white as snow. For fear of him the guards shook and became like dead men. But the angel said to the women, "Do not be afraid; I know that you are looking for Jesus who was crucified. He is not here; for he has been raised, as he said. Come, see the place where he lay. Then go quickly and tell his disciples, 'He has been raised from the dead, and indeed he is going ahead of you to Galilee; there you will see him.' This is my message for you."[110]

As God had entrusted the Davidic king to rule over his people, Israel, and as God had promised that a descendant of David would one day rule the world in justice and peace,[111] so Jesus is now granted the power to rule all creation on God's behalf.

And Jesus came and said to [his disciples], "All authority in heaven and on earth has been given to me."[112]

Still, before God's kingdom is visibly established, the word of the gospel must be proclaimed throughout the world, and disciples made of all nations.[113]

So the kingdom comes. But more must be said of the one who brings it[114] and of those who are to share in its glory.[115]

110. Matthew 28:1–7.
111. Isaiah 9:6–7; 11:1–5.
112. Matthew 28:18.
113. Matthew 28:19–20.
114. See chapter 6, below.
115. See chapter 7, below.

6

The Lord
of the Disciple

Whoever is not with me is against me, and whoever does not gather with me scatters.[1]

Though much that Jesus says and does in the Gospels invites our imitation, neither you nor I would be well advised to follow his lead in *this* text and announce to others that they simply cannot be indifferent to us. Most of us, it is true, begin life believing that we are the center of the universe. But most of us, it is to be hoped, have graduated to the stage of regretful maturity in which we concede that the majority of the people we see, and nearly all of the people we do not see, have no interest in, or even awareness of, our existence. Regrettably, too, they seem none the worse for the omission. Indifference to us appears, after all, to be a live option—indeed, the preferred option—for all but a few of our fellow human beings.

1. Matthew 12:30.

For or against Jesus

To be sure, there have always been people who have so forced themselves on public attention that most of their contemporaries can be said to be either for them or against them. Everyone in ancient Athens, it seems, knew of Socrates, and the question of whether his activities were good for society provoked sharply differing views. Napoleon polarized popular opinion in Europe in his day; so have several recent presidents of the United States. But the implication of Jesus' words is not that indifference to him is a circumstantial impossibility ("I am so well known and so controversial that people inevitably have an opinion about me") but that such indifference is morally impossible ("People are morally bound to be for me; they do wrong if they feign indifference, since their apparent indifference really amounts to opposing me").[2] An analogy may serve to illuminate the point.

Roberto works at a factory whose owners have just fired two employees unfairly. Ronald and Rhoda are organizing a protest, calling on all the workers at the factory to stop working at 11:00 the next morning. Roberto does not want to become involved; he simply wants to get on with his life. But whether he likes it or not, if Roberto remains at his work the next day, he will be doing his part to see that the protest fails. He must, it seems, be for or against what Rhoda and Ronald are doing.

> The implication of Jesus' words is not that indifference to him is a circumstantial impossibility but that such indifference is morally impossible.

Similarly, Jesus is saying that his mission is of a kind that people ought to support, and that failure to do so amounts to opposing it. Given Jesus' understanding of his mission, such a claim seems reasonable enough: if God is indeed putting things right in his universe, then people need to get in step with the divine agenda. At least two principles are at issue. For one thing, no one should be at cross-purposes with God. For another, to ignore Jesus' warning about the coming judgment and assume that life can continue

---

2. In the context, Jesus seems to be denying the possibility that critical statements that have just been made about him were offered from a position of detached neutrality.

as usual would be like disregarding a fire alarm. Where life itself is at stake, everyday business must take a secondary place.

So much seems clear. But Jesus' words appear to go even a step further than this. Rhoda and Ronald call on Roberto's support not for themselves as such, and certainly not for everything they do, but for a particular action that they are organizing. In Matthew 12:30, however, Jesus' words appear to demand a blanket *personal* support: "Whoever is not with me is against me." A number of other verses in the Gospel confirm that more than allegiance to Jesus' *mission* is at issue: people are to be willing to suffer at the hands of others for *Jesus'* sake,[3] to acknowledge their allegiance to *Jesus* even if it costs them their lives,[4] to love *Jesus* more than they love their nearest relations.[5] Words such as these, strange though they sound to modern ears, would hardly have been less strange in the ears of Jesus' contemporaries. Nowhere in the sacred scriptures of the Jews does a human being (prophet, priest, or king) demand personal allegiance like this.

God can, however, and does—at least in the Jewish scriptures. Elijah would not have dreamed of telling people that they must be for him or against him, but he does insist that they must choose whether to "follow" the Lord or Baal.[6] By implication, whoever is God *must* be followed. Moses summons people to show their allegiance not to himself but to the Lord, putting loyalty to God above the lives of their neighbors and kin.[7] People are not called upon to suffer for the sake of Moses, Elijah, or other mortals, but they suffer for the sake of God.[8] God is to be loved with *all* one's "heart," "soul," and "might."[9]

Admittedly, such demands remain strange for many of us even where God is concerned. We tend

> "Hear, O Israel: The LORD is our God, the LORD alone. You shall love the LORD your God with all your heart, and with all your soul, and with all your might."[10]

3. Matthew 5:11; 10:22, 24–25.
4. Matthew 10:32, 39.
5. Matthew 10:37.
6. 1 Kings 18:21.
7. Exodus 32:25–29; see also Deuteronomy 13:6–11.
8. Psalm 44:22; Jeremiah 15:15; 20:7–8.
9. Deuteronomy 6:5.
10. Deuteronomy 6:4–5.

to think of religion as merely *one* component in *some* people's lives: some people choose to be religious, among other things; others do not. By no means do even all of those who believe in God (or in gods) choose to be religious. To be religious is, for us, to carry out religious activities with some regularity—and people choose whether or not to do so. So widespread is indifference to religious activity in our society, and so dependent is its practice on personal choice, that one suspects many who indulge in such activity feel that they are showing God a favor when they do so. The thought-world of the Jewish scriptures, in which God rightly demands the absolute allegiance of his creatures, is far removed from the mental horizons of many of us in the modern West.

To understand the kind of allegiance that Jesus demands in Matthew's Gospel, then, we must begin with the notion of humanity's absolute duty toward God.

The Absolute Duty toward God

For many of us today, the only obligations that we are prepared to recognize are ones that we ourselves have undertaken, contracts of one kind or another that we ourselves have chosen to enter.[11] So essential is personal choice to our understanding of obligation that some people can imagine themselves free of responsibility for even the predictable consequences of their own actions if those consequences were not what they had in mind when they acted ("When I said I loved you, I didn't mean . . .")—rather like children playing chess who, when they realize the consequences of their choices, decide that they can "take back" their moves. Indeed, like that childhood ploy, we often think ourselves absolved even from responsibilities that we once freely undertook if we subsequently decide to choose differently. Resistant (at least at times) to the notion that we are bound by our own past choices, we are even less prepared to recognize obligations that we never chose.

---

11. Even our obligation to observe the laws of the land can be understood as fulfilling an implied contract: having chosen to live in a particular country, we are obliged to live by its laws.

Yet we, too, find ourselves in situations not of our choosing but in which most of us feel ourselves obligated. We did not choose our parents, but we rightly feel an obligation to care for them when they can no longer care for themselves. We rightly feel an obligation to share what we have with those less fortunate—perhaps recognizing that "but for the grace of God" we might be where they are. We regard as contemptible (and, by implication, wrong) people who disregard cries for help from those in obvious danger. Still, the myth by which many of us shape our lives is that we are self-made people, indebted to no one and therefore free to do as we please—and, moreover, that it is the duty of government to protect our inherent right to do so.

> The only obligations that many of us are prepared to recognize are ones that we ourselves have undertaken, contracts of one kind or another that we ourselves have chosen to enter.

The people who wrote the Bible thought very differently: we did not make our world, we did not make ourselves,[12] and we do not make the rules for either. In fundamental respects, it is not for us to choose what *is* good for ourselves, although we all must choose whether we will *do* what is good or what is evil.[13] All of us live in relationships with others; each relationship carries with it its own responsibilities.[14] To parents who brought us into the world and sustained us in our early lives, we are to give honor.[15] To our neighbors we are to show love and fair treatment, not giving false testimony against them or coveting what is theirs.[16]

> In fundamental respects—the writers of the Bible believed—it is not for us to choose what *is* good for ourselves, although we all must choose whether we will *do* what is good or what is evil.

For strangers, the poor, the orphan, and the widow we are to care.[17] And we are to fear, love, and worship God.[18]

---

12. Psalm 100:3.
13. See Proverbs 3:7.
14. See 1 Peter 2:17.
15. Exodus 20:12.
16. Leviticus 19:18; Exodus 20:16–17; 21:33–34; 22:5, 14–15.
17. Exodus 22:25–27; 23:9–12; Deuteronomy 10:19; 14:28–29; 15:7–11.
18. Deuteronomy 5:29; 6:5; 10:12–13, 20–21.

110   Understanding Matthew

The obligations under which we live are not arbitrarily imposed restraints on our freedom; rather, each is inherent in the relationships that, quite apart from our choosing, are a part of life on this earth. To grasp what it means to be a parent is to see that we owe our parents honor. To grasp what it means to be a neighbor is to see that we ought to treat our neighbors fairly. To grasp what it means to be poor or a stranger is to see that we ought to treat such people with compassion. To grasp what is meant by God is to see that God is due our love and worship. To fail in any of these areas is to fail to see what it means to be human or to live a truly human life.

> A proper human-God relationship is marked by a fear, a love, and a trust that differ, both qualitatively and quantitatively, from the fear, the love, and the trust that we can or should display toward any human being.

Our one absolute duty is toward God: God being *God*, it is in the nature of the case that our duty toward God is absolute. Just as a proper child-parent relationship is marked by an honor that is both peculiar and indispensable to that relationship, so a proper human-God relationship is marked by a fear, a love, and a trust that are indispensable to that relationship; and they differ, both qualitatively and quantitatively, from the fear, the love, and the trust that we can or should display toward any human being. God alone is to be *worshiped*, not simply because we have been told that we ought to worship God, but because God is *God*, and because we all live in God's presence and by God's goodness: to fail to worship God is to be blind to what is most basic about our existence. As it would simply be wrong to fail to acknowledge those who show us great kindness, so it is simply wrong to fail to acknowledge God. And as there is nature so awesome, art so beautiful, and athleticism so spectacular that they *command* our admiration, so the glory of God *commands* our worship. To fail to respond appropriately to what is good when we encounter it, or to the glory of God that surrounds us, is to show ourselves blind, foolish, or mean.

Absolute Duty in the Gospel

In the worldview of the Bible, humans, as humans, have an absolute duty toward God. Strikingly, in the Gospel of Matthew, Jesus commands the absolute obedience of those he encounters.[19]

If humans live by God's goodness, then to ignore God is to wrong him: one must be for or against God. Jesus (as we have seen) makes the same claim: "Whoever is not with me is against me." If humanity typically chooses to ignore or flout God's demands, then those who would be faithful to God are bound to suffer at the hands of others; Jesus prepares his disciples to suffer for *his* sake on precisely the same grounds.

Blessed are you when people revile you and persecute you and utter all kinds of evil against you falsely on my account. Rejoice and be glad, for your reward is great in heaven, for in the same way they persecuted the prophets who were before you.[20]

You will be hated by all because of my name. But the one who endures to the end will be saved.[21]

If loyalty to God must ultimately take precedence over all other loyalties, the same, Jesus claims, is true of the devotion due him.

He who loves father or mother more than me is not worthy of me; and he who loves son or daughter more than me is not worthy of me.[22]

If God is to be served even at the cost of one's life, the same is true of Jesus.

19. Dietrich Bonhoeffer made Matthew's point explicit in an address given in Barcelona in 1928: "I can doubtless live with or without Jesus as a religious genius, as an ethicist, as a gentleman—just as, after all, I can also live without Plato and Kant—all that has only relative meaning. Should, however, there be something in Christ that claims my life entirely with the full seriousness that here God himself speaks and if the word of God once became present only in Christ, then Christ has not only relative but absolute, urgent significance for me" (*A Testament to Freedom: The Essential Writings of Dietrich Bonhoeffer*, ed. Geffrey B. Kelly and F. Burton Nelson [San Francisco: Harper, 1990], 53).

20. Matthew 5:11–12.

21. Matthew 10:22. See also 10:18; 19:29; 24:9.

22. Matthew 10:37 RSV.

He who does not take his cross and follow me is not worthy of me. He who finds his life will lose it, and he who loses his life for my sake will find it.[23]

God alone is to be worshiped; yet worship is given to Jesus.[24] The faith that only God is due is appropriately placed in Jesus.[25] People are to "come to" Jesus just as God is to be "sought."[26] And Jesus, in a blanket way that is true of God but inappropriate in the case of any mere human being, is to be "followed."[27]

> In the worldview of the Bible, humans, as humans, have an absolute duty toward God. Strikingly, in the Gospel of Matthew, Jesus commands the absolute obedience of those he encounters.

That Jesus is due the absolute obedience, love, and trust to which God alone can lay claim is consistent with the divine functions that Jesus assumes in the Gospel.[28] On his own authority,[29] Jesus declares how people must live if they are to enter the kingdom of God;[30] yet both telling others how they ought to live and spelling out the conditions for admission to God's kingdom would seem to be God's prerogatives.[31]

---

23. Matthew 10:38–39 RSV. NRSV substitutes "whoever" and "they" for "he," recognizing that Jesus' words apply equally to female and male disciples. In substituting "take up the cross" for "take his cross," however, it depersonalizes a summons that in Matthew's Greek text is strikingly personal.

24. Matthew 14:33; 28:9, 17. Compare 4:10. The same verb is used a number of times elsewhere in the Gospel of reverence shown toward Jesus (2:2, 8, 11; 8:2; 9:18; 15:25; 20:20); where homage ends and worship begins is left unspecified.

25. For example, Matthew 8:5–13; 9:20–22, 27–30; 18:6. Compare Psalm 118:8–9; Isaiah 31:1–3.

26. Isaiah 55:6; Matthew 11:28.

27. 1 Kings 18:21; Matthew 10:38; 16:24.

28. Note that Matthew understands the "LORD" of Isaiah 40:3 to refer to Jesus (Matthew 3:3; see also 11:10). And can the "kingdom" of the "Son of Man" (= Jesus; see the discussion below) in 13:41 and 16:28 be distinguished from the kingdom of God? (See also Matthew 20:21.)

29. Note the words repeated six times in Matthew 5: "But I say to you" (5:22, 28, 32, 34, 39, 44); also the frequently repeated formula "Truly I tell you" (for example, 5:18, 26; 6:2, 5, 16; 8:10). According to 7:28–29, the authority with which Jesus spoke astonished his listeners.

30. For example, Matthew 5:20; 7:13–14, 21.

31. Note, too, the claim that Jesus' own words will endure when the words of God's law itself will pass away (Matthew 24:35; compare 5:18).

Forgiveness can only be granted by one who has been wronged (it is not, for example, for me to forgive you if you steal from your pharmacist) *and* by God, against whose goodness every wrongdoing is an offense; yet Jesus pronounces the forgiveness of sins.[32] If God alone knows our hearts, God alone can be our judge; yet Jesus, the "Son of Man,"[33] will judge all humankind.[34] God alone can save from sin; yet this, Matthew tells us, is Jesus' mission.[35]

Jesus, God's "Son"

Still, Jesus is obviously distinguished from God throughout the Gospel.[36] He prays to God,[37] speaks about God,[38] and is even spoken about *by* God.[39] In each case it is clear that he is talking neither to nor about himself. Nor, to be sure, is Jesus setting himself up as a rival to God, a kind of second deity: only one God is due our absolute obedience, love, and trust.[40]

One cannot say that the mystery of Jesus' mission—he assumes the prerogatives of God yet is distinguished from God—is ever resolved in early Christian literature. But the Gospel of Matthew, like other early Christian literature, has a name for Jesus' unique nature: he is God's "Son."[41] As God's Son he is distinct from the God who is his Father, yet free to speak on his Father's behalf and to claim the same allegiance that is due his Father.[42] Since God has chosen to act on earth in the person of God's Son, those who

32. Matthew 9:2; note the reaction of "some of the scribes" in 9:3.

33. The significance of this title will be discussed later in this chapter.

34. Matthew 7:22–23; 16:27; 25:31–46.

35. Psalm 130:8; Matthew 1:21.

36. The point of Matthew 19:17, however, is not to distinguish between Jesus and God (as though Jesus were not good though God is!) but to say that God, who is good, has already indicated in his law what the good is that he requires; there is, then, no reason to raise the issue now as though it still needed to be resolved.

37. For example, Matthew 11:25–26; 14:23.

38. Matthew 5:8–9 and throughout the Gospel.

39. Matthew 3:17; 17:5.

40. Matthew 6:24, 33; 22:37–38. Jesus himself submits to his Father's will (26:39, 42).

41. Matthew 2:15; 3:17; 14:33, and elsewhere.

42. Note how, in Psalm 2, rebellion against God's "Son" (the anointed king) is rebellion against God.

acknowledge God must acknowledge his Son. It is, indeed, only through the Son that God is known, and only through enlightenment from God that the Son is recognized for who he is.

> At that time Jesus said, "I thank you, Father, Lord of heaven and earth, because you have hidden these things from the wise and the intelligent and have revealed them to infants; yes, Father, for such was your gracious will. All things have been handed over to me by my Father; and no one knows the Son except the Father, and no one knows the Father except the Son and anyone to whom the Son chooses to reveal him."[43]

> [Jesus] said to [his disciples], "But who do you say that I am?" Simon Peter answered, "You are the Messiah, the Son of the living God." And Jesus answered him, "Blessed are you, Simon son of Jonah! For flesh and blood has not revealed this to you, but my Father in heaven."[44]

Three observations are in order here.

1. In the quotation just given, "Son of God" appears to be an equivalent of "Messiah": "You are the Messiah, the Son of the living God." Equating the two terms seems a natural development from texts in the Jewish scriptures. God had said that he would be "a father" to the Davidic king in Israel and the king would be a "son" to God;[45] that is, God would care for the king as a father cares for his son, the king would owe God a son's obedience, and the king's subjects must show

> As God's Son, Jesus is distinct from the God who is his Father, yet free to speak on his Father's behalf and to claim the same allegiance that is due his Father.

their ruler something of the deference due God. The same promise would presumably apply to the Messiah, the descendant of David and coming king; it is not surprising, then, that "God's Son" could be used as a title for the Messiah. On the other hand, Jews thought of the Messiah as a *human* king who would be endowed with God's Spirit.[46] Jesus goes beyond what was expected of the Messiah in assuming divine prerogatives; indeed, he insists that

43. Matthew 11:25–27.
44. Matthew 16:15–17.
45. 2 Samuel 7:14.
46. See Isaiah 11:1–2.

the Messiah is David's "Lord."[47] In Matthew's Gospel, then, "God's Son" must mean a good deal more than "Messiah"—at least as "Messiah" was traditionally understood.

2. In Matthew's Gospel, God has many children, but Jesus is unique. The disciples are to live as children of God, patterning their behavior after that of their Father in heaven.[48] They are to seek reward from their Father in heaven, pray to their Father in heaven, trust their heavenly Father to know and provide for their needs.[49] In what sense is God their "Father"? To speak of God in this way is to take language from a familiar human relationship and apply it by analogy to a human relationship with God. The disciples thus know God as their "Father" in that he cares for them, provides for them, and tells them what to do.[50] The same father-child analogy is used in the case of Jesus, but here it implies (as we have seen) much more. As God's Son, Jesus speaks with God's authority. And Jesus is given the love, trust, obedience, and even worship that are due God himself.

> In Matthew's Gospel, "God's Son" means a good deal more than "Messiah"—at least as "Messiah" was traditionally understood.

A minor detail in Matthew's Gospel underlines the difference between Jesus as God's Son and the disciples, who are also (but in a different sense) "children" of God. Jesus speaks repeatedly of God as "my Father," indicating the relationship he has with God as his "Son."[51] And he speaks repeatedly of God to his disciples as "your Father," indicating the relationship they have with God as his "children."[52] But Jesus never speaks of God to his disciples as "our Father," as he would if his relationship with God were the same as theirs. A group of *disciples* may address God as "our Father in heaven."[53] But when Jesus is involved, the

---

47. Matthew 22:41–45. See the discussion under the heading "David" in chapter 4, above.

48. Matthew 5:45.

49. Matthew 6:1, 9, 32–33.

50. Note that the analogy is made explicit in Matthew 7:11.

51. For example, Matthew 7:21; 10:32–33; 11:27; 12:50. See also 16:27; 25:34.

52. For example, Matthew 5:16, 45, 48; 6:1, 8, 14–15. The singular "your" is used in 6:4, 6, 18.

53. Matthew 6:9.

relationships are distinguished: God is "my Father" and "your Father" but not "our Father."[54]

3. The Gospel of Matthew (a) ascribes to Jesus divine pre-rogatives, (b) distinguishes Jesus from God, and (c) calls Jesus God's (unique) Son; but it is not concerned to speculate about *how* Jesus could be both identified with God and distinguished from God or what kind of "nature" he had. For Matthew, it is essential that Jesus is approached and served with the devotion due God alone; it has not yet become important, however, to spell out what this implies about the nature of Jesus—or, for that matter, of God. Later Christian tradition, for which Matthew's Gospel was authoritative Scripture, developed creeds to express and safeguard the various aspects of the mystery:

[I believe] in one Lord Jesus Christ, the only-begotten Son of God, begotten of his Father before all worlds, God of God, Light of Light, very God of very God, Begotten, not made, being of one substance with the Father, by whom all things were made; who for us men and for our salvation came down from heaven and was incarnate by the Holy Spirit of the virgin Mary, and was made man. . . .[55]

> For Matthew, it is essential that Jesus is approached and served with the devotion due God alone; it has not yet become important, however, to spell out what this implies about the nature of Jesus—or, for that matter, of God.

In the Gospel of Matthew, only a single verse attempts a formula that both respects the unity of God (God *is* one) and reflects the convictions that God is truly present in the person of Jesus and in the Spirit that empowers both Jesus and his disciples:[56] new disciples are to be baptized "in the name of the Father and of the Son and of the Holy Spirit."[57] In formulas such as this[58] we can see the roots of later Christian understandings

---

54. Compare John 20:17.

55. Nicene Creed.

56. Matthew 28:19. For the Spirit, see Matthew 3:16; 4:1; 10:20; 12:18, 28.

57. Note also that in Matthew 3:16–17, the Spirit descends on Jesus, who is then declared to be God's "Son" by his Father in heaven; the three "persons" of what would later be called the Trinity are all present here; but a trinitarian formula is not used.

58. See also 2 Corinthians 13:13.

of God as Trinity.[59] Yet the Gospel of Matthew itself must be seen as providing the raw material on which later creeds were based rather than as a narrative designed to illustrate the truth of an existing doctrine or creed.

Jesus, the "Son of Man"

Before we leave the subject of Jesus' identity in Matthew's Gospel, something needs to be said about Jesus' favorite designation for himself in the Gospel: he is the "Son of Man."[60] A "son of man," in Hebrew idiom, is simply a human being.

> When I look at thy heavens, the work of thy fingers,
>   the moon and the stars which thou hast established,
> what is man that thou art mindful of him,
>   and the son of man that thou dost care for him?[61]

When Ezekiel is repeatedly addressed by God as "son of man," the point is presumably to stress the infinite gap between the God who speaks and the human who receives and communicates

59. Although earthly analogies to the divine Trinity were sometimes offered (for example, the flame, light, and warmth of a fire may all be distinguished; but each is indispensable to, and inseparable from, the one fire, and each may be referred to as "the fire"), the formulations that spoke of God as Trinity were not thought to make God comprehensible. They served merely to safeguard the mystery of God as Christians believed God had revealed himself: God is one, but the Jesus whom Christians worshiped, the Father to whose will Jesus submitted, and the Spirit whose presence they sensed in their midst must all be acknowledged as God.

In a circular letter sent out to his beleaguered former seminarians for Christmas 1939, Bonhoeffer wrote: "Without the holy night there is no theology. 'God revealed in the flesh,' the God-man Jesus Christ, is the holy mystery which theology is appointed to guard. What a mistake to think that it is the task of theology to unravel God's mystery, to bring it down to the flat, ordinary human wisdom of experience and reason! It is the task of theology solely to preserve God's wonder as wonder, to understand, to defend, to glorify God's mystery as mystery. This and nothing else was the intention of the ancient church when it fought with unflagging zeal over the mystery of the persons of the Trinity and the natures of Jesus Christ" (*A Testament to Freedom: The Essential Writings of Dietrich Bonhoeffer*, ed. Geffrey B. Kelly and F. Burton Nelson [San Francisco: Harper, 1990], 472).

60. That Jesus uses "Son of Man" to refer to himself is clear from a comparison of Matthew 8:19 and 20; 16:13 and 15; 24:3 and 27; 26:21 and 24; and 26:45 and 46.

61. Psalm 8:3–4 RSV.

God's message.[62] At times Jesus speaks of himself as "the Son of Man" in contexts in which he appears very human indeed.

> Foxes have holes, and birds of the air have nests; but the Son of Man has nowhere to lay his head.[63]

> The Son of Man came eating and drinking, and they say, "Look, a glutton and a drunkard, a friend of tax collectors and sinners!"[64]

Still, humans do not generally make a point of emphasizing to which species they belong. There is something unusual, even labored, about Jesus' use of the expression:[65] repeatedly "The Son of Man has . . ." or "The Son of Man came . . ." simply means "*I* have . . ." or "*I* came . . ." We may suspect that the labored insistence on the humanness of Jesus among contemporaries for whom his humanness was not in doubt contains in itself a suggestion that this is a human with a difference. The suspicion is confirmed by a number of sayings that ascribe to "the Son of Man" divine roles, power, and glory.

> At times Jesus speaks of himself as "the Son of Man" in contexts in which he appears very human indeed.

> The Son of Man will send his angels, and they will collect out of his kingdom all causes of sin and all evildoers.[66]

> For the Son of Man is to come with his angels in the glory of his Father, and then he will repay everyone for what has been done.[67]

> They will see "the Son of Man coming on the clouds of heaven" with power and great glory.[68]

62. Ezekiel 2:1, 3, 6, 8; 3:1, 3, 4, and elsewhere. (The NRSV renders the expression "O mortal.")
63. Matthew 8:20.
64. Matthew 11:19.
65. That the expression was thought unusual but typical of Jesus' speech is suggested by its ubiquity in his sayings in all four New Testament Gospels and its virtual absence elsewhere in the New Testament.
66. Matthew 13:41.
67. Matthew 16:27.
68. Matthew 24:30.

Lurking in the background of such texts are words from a well-known vision in the Jewish scriptures:

> I saw in the night visions,
>> and behold, with the clouds of heaven
>> there came *one like a son of man*,
> and he came to the Ancient of Days
> and was presented before him.
> And to him was given dominion
>> and glory and kingdom,
> that all peoples, nations, and languages
>> should serve him;
> his dominion is an everlasting dominion,
>> which shall not pass away,
> and his kingdom one
>> that shall not be destroyed.[69]

To *this* human being belong eternal power, glory, and kingship. Jesus' use of the expression "Son of Man" allows him not only to allude to the vision in Daniel but also to make indirect claim to be the one who will fulfill it.

But the claim is indirect: not "I" explicitly but "the Son of Man" will come with power and glory. The glorious King who will one day establish God's kingdom is, for those with eyes to see it, the "Son of Man"—the human being whom you see before you. In the very designation that Jesus most frequently uses of himself is contained the offense that is inherent in his mission.

> Jesus' use of the expression "Son of Man" allows him not only to allude to the vision in Daniel but also to make indirect claim to be the one who will fulfill it.

---

69. Daniel 7:13–14 RSV.

7

The Life
of the Disciple

Then Jesus told his disciples, "If any want to become my followers, let them deny themselves and take up their cross and follow me."[1]

A stranger invitation you will never read. Instinctively human beings desire to live long, to do what they themselves choose to do, to experience as little pain as possible. Jesus invites us to deny these human instincts and to join him on a path that leads to a Roman cross. "When Christ calls a man, he bids him come and die."[2] Strange that he should find any takers. Strange that he *has* found many takers.

But not so strange, after all, in the context of Matthew's Gospel. If we keep Matthew's basic convictions in mind, we can make some sense even of his call to discipleship.

1. Matthew 16:24.
2. Dietrich Bonhoeffer, *The Cost of Discipleship*, trans. R. H. Fuller, abridged trans. (New York: Macmillan, 1963), 99. (Less epigrammatically, the more recent translation of Bonhoeffer's words reads, "Whenever Christ calls us, his call leads us to death" [Dietrich Bonhoeffer, *Discipleship*, trans. B. Green and R. Krauss (Minneapolis: Fortress, 2001), 87].)

Our lives, Matthew believes, are not an accident that happens in a world that happens to be; we live and are sustained through life by the goodness of God, our heavenly Father. God made us out of love and made us to love: to respond to his own infinite love with a love for him that engages all our heart, soul, and mind. Moreover, hearts given in love to God can harbor no ill will toward other human beings; all must be embraced in love.[3] Such, for Matthew, is the good life—a life lived in harmony with Goodness.

Yet the world must now be reclaimed for Goodness, since the path it has chosen is decidedly not that of love but rather of self-assertion reflected in ubiquitous outbursts of anger, cutting remarks, and acts of murder;[4] in treating sexual gratification as a necessity and love as a (very dispensable) option;[5] in irreverent pledges of part-time honesty;[6] in defending every inch of one's imagined rights against any who dare to encroach upon them;[7] in reciprocal loves and reciprocal hatreds;[8] in making personal wealth one's god;[9] in greatness measured in power exercised at the expense of the weak.[10] In such a world, calls to goodness are quickly suppressed, and intrusions of goodness quickly snuffed out.[11]

> The mission of Jesus is to reclaim the world for Goodness *by* goodness. Love can only triumph through love.

The mission of Jesus is to reclaim the world for Goodness *by* goodness. All the powers of Goodness are at his disposal, and they exceed by far the forces of evil; but love can only triumph through love. Thus, when Jesus proclaims the approach of God's kingdom, he invites all to share in its glories, but he pressures no one. He employs God's power to heal the sick and set free the oppressed, but he refuses to exploit the same power to compel allegiance

---

3. Matthew 5:43–48; 22:34–40.
4. Matthew 5:21–22.
5. Matthew 5:27–28.
6. Matthew 5:33–37.
7. Matthew 5:38–42.
8. Matthew 5:43–48.
9. Matthew 6:24.
10. Matthew 20:25.
11. For example, Matthew 5:10–12; 10:16–25; 17:10–13.

from those disinclined to believe. He pronounces those blessed who are not offended ("put off") by his humble appearance, but he does not transform his appearance[12] to compel belief from those who choose to take offense. Meek and mild with many, he bears himself very differently with those who oppose him and lead others astray, denouncing their sin and threatening judgment.[13] But rousing the endangered is itself an act of love;[14] and in the face of opposition, Jesus refuses to save himself from death, giving his own life to gain forgiveness for others. Paradoxically, love triumphs over evil by allowing itself to be overcome *by* evil.

It would be no triumph, to be sure, had the love that proved faithful unto death not emerged triumphant from the grave.[15] Without Easter Matthew would not be a "gospel" ("good news") but simply a tragedy of deluded innocence snuffed out by the corruption it quixotically challenged. *Everything* in Matthew hinges on the truth of the claims that Goodness—not chaos, indifference, or evil—lies at the source of all life, that Goodness must therefore prevail in the end, and that Jesus is the One through whom divine Goodness reclaims its creation. Jesus' death, then, marks not the end but a stage in the establishment of God's kingdom. He rises from the dead and will some day return—when the good news of the kingdom has been brought to all the earth, and disciples won from all nations—to seal the eternal triumph of the good.

> *Everything* in Matthew hinges on the truth of the claims that Goodness—not chaos, indifference, or evil—lies at the source of all life, that Goodness must therefore prevail in the end, and that Jesus is the One through whom divine Goodness reclaims its creation.

---

12. Matthew 17:1–8 records such a transformation: Jesus was "transfigured . . . , and his face shone like the sun, and his clothes became dazzling white. . . . Suddenly a bright cloud overshadowed [Jesus and his disciples], and from the cloud a voice said, 'This is my Son, the Beloved; with him I am well pleased; listen to him!'" But the vision is seen only by Jesus' three closest disciples; and they themselves are told (verse 9) to say nothing about it "until after the Son of Man has been raised from the dead."

13. Matthew 12:22–42; 15:1–9; 21:12–13; 23:13–36.

14. Even the sharp denunciations of Matthew 23 must be read in the light of 23:37–39.

15. Matthew 28:1–10.

In the meantime, Jesus' disciples must live in the world that crucified their Lord; they can expect no better treatment themselves.

> A disciple is not above his teacher, nor a servant above his master; it is enough for the disciple to be like his teacher, and the servant like his master. If they have called the master of the house Beelzebul,[16] how much more will they malign those of his household.[17]

> Jesus' call to discipleship is thus a summons to share, for the love of Goodness, in the fate of goodness in the world.

Jesus' call to discipleship is thus a summons to share, for the love of Goodness, in the fate of goodness in the world—with the assurance that the world does not have the last word.

The Gospel of Matthew tells the story of Jesus, but it is meant to inspire its readers to a life of discipleship. In this chapter we will highlight a few important aspects of the disciple's life, as portrayed in Matthew's Gospel.

Obeying the Master

Disciples, by definition, submit to their master's instructions. Jesus, as we have seen,[18] calls his disciples to live without worry, trusting God, their heavenly Father, to supply their needs; to devote themselves to serving God, not to accumulating wealth; to live by the standard of God's goodness; to be prepared to forgive all who wrong them, as they themselves have been granted God's forgiveness.

Of the many other areas in which Jesus instructs his disciples in Matthew's Gospel, we here note three.

1. Jesus insists that his disciples do their acts of kindness or piety for God's eyes alone, not to impress other people.[19] Typically, Jesus makes his point with graphic illustrations.

16. That is, Satan; see Matthew 9:34; 12:24–28.
17. Matthew 10:24–25 RSV.
18. See chapters 2 and 3, above.
19. Matthew 6:1.

So whenever you give alms, do not sound a trumpet before you, as the hypocrites do in the synagogues and in the streets, so that they may be praised by others. Truly I tell you, they have received their reward. But when you give alms, do not let your left hand know what your right hand is doing, so that your alms may be done in secret; and your Father who sees in secret will reward you.

And whenever you pray, do not be like the hypocrites; for they love to stand and pray in the synagogues and at the street corners, so that they may be seen by others. Truly I tell you, they have received their reward. But whenever you pray, go into your room and shut the door and pray to your Father who is in secret; and your Father who sees in secret will reward you. . . .

> Jesus insists that his disciples do their acts of kindness or piety for God's eyes alone.

And whenever you fast, do not look dismal, like the hypocrites, for they disfigure their faces so as to show others that they are fasting. Truly I tell you, they have received their reward. But when you fast, put oil on your head and wash your face, so that your fasting may be seen not by others but by your Father who is in secret; and your Father who sees in secret will reward you.[20]

2. Love makes it its business to serve others; it has no desire to be served. Greatness in the kingdom of Love is measured in service, not in power.

You know that the rulers of the Gentiles lord it over them, and their great ones are tyrants over them. It will not be so among you; but whoever wishes to be great among you must be your servant, and whoever wishes to be first among you must be your slave; just as the Son of Man came not to be served but to serve, and to give his life a ransom for many.[21]

> Greatness in the kingdom of Love is measured in service, not in power.

If the way of the world is to seek greatness in power, the path to *God's* kingdom lies in becoming like children: power*less*, insignificant in the eyes of other people, though precious in the eyes of God.

At that time the disciples came to Jesus and asked, "Who is the greatest in the kingdom of heaven?" He called a child, whom he

---

20. Matthew 6:2–6, 16–18.
21. Matthew 20:25–28. See also 23:11–12.

put among them, and said, "Truly I tell you, unless you change and become like children, you will never enter the kingdom of heaven. Whoever becomes humble like this child is the greatest in the kingdom of heaven. Whoever welcomes one such child in my name welcomes me. . . .

"Take care that you do not despise one of these little ones; for, I tell you, in heaven their angels continually see the face of my Father in heaven."[22]

Then little children were being brought to him in order that he might lay his hands on them and pray. The disciples spoke sternly to those who brought them; but Jesus said, "Let the little children come to me, and do not stop them; for it is to such as these that the kingdom of heaven belongs." And he laid his hands on them.[23]

> Children of God show their dependence on God and their trust in him by coming to God in prayer.

3. Children of God can be sure that their heavenly Father knows their needs before they even mention them. Nonetheless, children of God show their dependence on God and their trust in him by coming to God in prayer. No treatment of discipleship in Matthew would be complete without mention of the disciples' prayer.

Pray then in this way:
Our Father in heaven,
    hallowed be your name.
    Your kingdom come.
    Your will be done,
        on earth as it is in heaven.
Give us this day our daily bread.
And forgive us our debts,
    as we also have forgiven our debtors.
And do not bring us to the time of trial,
    but rescue us from the evil one.[24]

22. Matthew 18:1–5, 10.
23. Matthew 19:13–15.
24. Matthew 6:9–13. Matthew leaves the prayer without a conclusion. In copies later made of his Gospel, a suitable ending is added: "For the kingdom and the power and the glory are yours forever. Amen." (See the footnote to Matthew 6:13 in the NRSV.)

If Gentiles "heap up empty phrases" when they pray, "think[ing] that they will be heard because of their many words,"[25] children assured of their heavenly Father's goodwill may approach him with words both confident and to the point.[26] Their first concern, however, is for God's own glory. It grieves them that the name of their Father is treated with contempt, that the rule of Love is despised, that the commands of Love are flouted. They pray first, then, that the day will come soon when these conditions will be reversed: God's name will be held sacred, his rule universally acknowledged, his will everywhere done. The requests imply, of course, the disciples' willingness to hallow God's name in their own lives, to submit to God's rule themselves, and to obey God's will.

Disciples who seek to please God rather than pursue personal wealth and who trust God to watch over all their tomorrows are content to ask only for provision of what they need for today ("our daily bread"). Aware of their many failings, they ask God for forgiveness, acknowledging that the request can be granted only to those prepared to forgive others. Recognizing their weakness and their proneness to stumble, they ask God to keep them from falling when their faith is tried and to deliver them from every attack of the evil one. All these prayers are offered in the assurance that God, their heavenly Father, will give what is good to all who ask him.[27]

Following the Master

If Jesus were only a teacher of righteousness, then adopting his instructions as one's way of life might exhaust the responsibilities of discipleship. But if Jesus is Love reclaiming the world, then

25. Matthew 6:7.
26. "Genuine prayer . . . is never demonstrative, neither before God nor before ourselves, nor before others. If God did not know what I need, then I would have to think about *how* I should tell God, *what* I should tell God, *whether* I should tell God. But the faith out of which I am praying prevents such reflecting or demonstrating" (Bonhoeffer, *Discipleship* [2001], 153).
27. Matthew 7:11.

| If Jesus is Love reclaiming the world, then discipleship entails personal allegiance to him. |

discipleship entails personal allegiance to him.[28] Obeying his instructions remains an indispensable aspect of one's allegiance; but the essence of discipleship is devotion to the Master. For some, such devotion means abandoning their occupations, family ties, and possessions in order to be with Jesus.

> Everyone who has left houses or brothers or sisters or father or mother or children or fields, for my name's sake, will receive a hundredfold, and will inherit eternal life.[29]

For all, it means a willingness to show loyalty to Jesus even if it divides them from their closest kin, and even if it costs life itself.

> He who loves father or mother more than me is not worthy of me; and he who loves son or daughter more than me is not worthy of me; and he who does not take his cross and follow me is not worthy of me. He who finds his life will lose it, and he who loses his life for my sake will find it.[30]

No one becomes a disciple on their own initiative, deciding that—all things considered—a life of discipleship is the best of the available options. The initiative always lies with Jesus: Jesus *calls* people he encounters to come and follow him. Disciples sense at once that they must obey what he says; without further ado, they follow.[31]

> As he walked by the Sea of Galilee, he saw two brothers, Simon, who is called Peter, and Andrew his brother, casting a net into the sea—for

28. See the discussion in chapter 6, above, about the absolute duty of humans toward God and about absolute duty in Matthew.
29. Matthew 19:29. See also 4:18–22; 9:9; 19:27.
30. Matthew 10:37–39 RSV.
31. "Things used to be different. Then they could live quietly in the country, unnoticed in their work, keep the law, and wait for the Messiah. But now he was there; now his call came. Now faith no longer meant keeping quiet and waiting, but going in discipleship with him. Now his call to discipleship dissolved all ties for the sake of the unique commitment to Jesus Christ. Now all bridges had to be burned and the step taken to enter into endless insecurity, in order to know what Jesus demands and what Jesus gives" (Bonhoeffer, *Discipleship* [2001], 62).

they were fishermen. And he said to them, "Follow me, and I will make you fish for people." Immediately they left their nets and followed him. As he went from there, he saw two other brothers, James son of Zebedee and his brother John, in the boat with their father Zebedee, mending their nets, and he called them. Immediately they left the boat and their father, and followed him.[32]

The call, to be sure, goes out to all.[33] Those who live in Love's world apart from Love can only find life wearying and burdensome, and Jesus offers rest.

Come to me, all you that are weary and are carrying heavy burdens, and I will give you rest. Take my yoke upon you, and learn from me; for I am gentle and humble in heart, and you will find rest for your souls. For my yoke is easy, and my burden is light.[34]

But—as the Gospel shows repeatedly—only those with ears open to hear the invitation respond and become disciples.

The life to which disciples are called is, above all, a life in Jesus' presence—no less for those who live after Easter than for those who follow him in the pages of the Gospel.

> The life to which disciples are called is, above all, a life in Jesus' presence.

Where two or three are gathered in my name, I am there among them.[35]

And remember, I am with you always, to the end of the age.[36]

In whatever storms they find themselves, in whatever crises Jesus summons them to enter, Jesus himself is close at hand and offers his protection.

Immediately [Jesus] made the disciples get into the boat and go on ahead to the other side. . . . When evening came, he was there alone,

32. Matthew 4:18–22.
33. See the discussion in chapter 5, above, under the heading "The Invitation to God's Kingdom."
34. Matthew 11:28–30.
35. Matthew 18:20.
36. Matthew 28:20.

but by this time the boat, battered by the waves, was far from the land, for the wind was against them. And early in the morning he came walking toward them on the sea. But when the disciples saw him walking on the sea, they were terrified, saying, "It is a ghost!" And they cried out in fear. But immediately Jesus spoke to them and said, "Take heart, it is I; do not be afraid."

Peter answered him, "Lord, if it is you, command me to come to you on the water." He said, "Come." So Peter got out of the boat, started walking on the water, and came toward Jesus. But when he noticed the strong wind, he became frightened, and beginning to sink, he cried out, "Lord, save me!" Jesus immediately reached out his hand and caught him, saying to him, "You of little faith, why did you doubt?" When they got into the boat, the wind ceased. And those in the boat worshiped him, saying, "Truly you are the Son of God."[37]

Peter's faltering faith is typical of the disciples' conduct throughout the Gospel: to be with Jesus is inevitably to fail Jesus, good intentions notwithstanding.

Then Jesus said to [his disciples], "You will all become deserters because of me this night; for it is written,
　'I will strike the shepherd,
　　and the sheep of the flock will be scattered.'
But after I am raised up, I will go ahead of you to Galilee." Peter said to him, "Though all become deserters because of you, I will never desert you." Jesus said to him, "Truly I tell you, this very night, before the cock crows, you will deny me three times." Peter said to him, "Even though I must die with you, I will not deny you." And so said all the disciples.[38]

At Jesus' arrest, all his disciples flee.[39] Peter promptly proceeds to deny—three times—any acquaintance with Jesus.[40] Yet it is the same group of disciples, with Peter at their lead, who are later entrusted with the task of making "disciples of all nations."[41] Jesus' patience with those who follow him seems endless.

And to them Jesus promises a place in God's kingdom. The Sermon on the Mount begins with Jesus blessing his disciples,

37. Matthew 14:22–33. See also 8:23–27.
38. Matthew 26:31–35.
39. Matthew 26:56.
40. Matthew 26:69–75.
41. Matthew 28:18–20.

offering them consolation that is at the same time a checklist of what it means to follow Jesus.

> Blessed are the poor in spirit, for theirs is the kingdom of heaven.
> Blessed are those who mourn, for they will be comforted.
> Blessed are the meek, for they will inherit the earth.
> Blessed are those who hunger and thirst for righteousness, for they will be filled.
> Blessed are the merciful, for they will receive mercy.
> Blessed are the pure in heart, for they will see God.
> Blessed are the peacemakers, for they will be called children of God.
> Blessed are those who are persecuted for righteousness' sake, for theirs is the kingdom of heaven.
> Blessed are you when people revile you and persecute you and utter all kinds of evil against you falsely on my account. Rejoice and be glad, for your reward is great in heaven, for in the same way they persecuted the prophets who were before you.[42]

The Sermon on the Mount begins with Jesus blessing his disciples, offering them consolation that is at the same time a checklist of what it means to follow Jesus.

The "poor in spirit" are those who find life wearying and burdensome but who come to Jesus to find rest. "Those who mourn" are those grieved by a world gone wrong and by their own part in its waywardness; grieved afresh by every sin against Goodness and grieved continuously by the frightful toll to be paid in a world where the life of goodness is rejected. The "meek" are those who renounce the world's pursuit of power, become like children, serve others, and bear their abuse. "Those who hunger and thirst for righteousness" are those who long to be good as God their Father is good and who long to see his goodness prevail everywhere on earth. The "merciful" are those instinctively ready to help all who are in need, quick to forgive all who do them wrong,

42. Matthew 5:3–12.

and far too aware of their own failings to condemn the faults of others. The "pure in heart" are those who devote themselves single-mindedly to God and his service. The "peacemakers" are those who respond to evil with kindness rather than insist on their rights or strive to get even. Though the life of goodness lived by the poor in spirit, the meek, the merciful, the pure in heart, and the peacemakers may provoke opposition on earth, its reward is the kingdom of heaven.

The Community of Disciples

Disciples are made one by one as people hear the call of Jesus and resolve to follow him. As disciples, they remain individually responsible before God for every thought they think, every look they cast, every word they speak, and their every deed. Nonetheless, to be a disciple of Jesus is also to join the company of others who follow him. Jesus' disciples formed a kind of community already during his lifetime; even more markedly they constituted a community after his resurrection. Jesus was building his *church*.

> To be a disciple of Jesus is to join the company of others who follow him.

Now when Jesus came into the district of Caesarea Philippi, he asked his disciples, "Who do people say that the Son of Man is?" And they said, "Some say John the Baptist, but others Elijah, and still others Jeremiah or one of the prophets." He said to them, "But who do you say that I am?" Simon Peter answered, "You are the Messiah, the Son of the living God." And Jesus answered him, "Blessed are you, Simon son of Jonah! For flesh and blood has not revealed this to you, but my Father in heaven. And I tell you, you are Peter, and on this rock[43]

43. The Greek form of "Peter" (*Petros*) is very close to the word used here for "rock" (*petra*). Clearly, a play on words is intended, although over the centuries interpreters have disagreed about the identity of the "rock" on which the church is to be built. For some (perhaps influenced by the insistence of 1 Corinthians 3:11 that the only foundation for the church is Jesus Christ), the rock is Christ; for others, it is the confession just made by Peter that Jesus is the Christ. Others agree that the reference is to Peter himself but disagree about what this means. For some, Peter is mentioned solely as a representative figure for all the disciples (that is, all who confess, as Peter did, that Jesus is "the Messiah, the Son of the living God"). Others see Peter's significance as

I will build my church, and the gates of Hades will not prevail against it. I will give you the keys of the kingdom of heaven, and whatever you bind on earth will be bound in heaven, and whatever you loose on earth will be loosed in heaven."[44]

The new community, these verses imply, is distinguished in the first place by its confession that Jesus is "the Messiah, the Son of the living God." It cannot but provoke opposition from those who have long since rejected God's rule; yet not even the powers of darkness can prevail against it. As people respond to the Messiah's church and its witness to God's kingdom, they respond to the Messiah himself. This response will prove decisive when the Messiah returns and God's kingdom is established.[45]

Matthew's story is the story of Jesus, not that of the post-Easter church. We may nonetheless note a few aspects of what the Gospel reveals about Matthew's understanding of the latter community.

1. Those who become disciples are baptized "in the name of the Father and of the Son and of the Holy Spirit."[46] Readers of Matthew's Gospel first encounter baptism in connection with John the Baptist:[47] John baptizes those who repent and confess their sins in order to prepare themselves for God's kingdom. Baptism in the church carries the same meaning, but the baptized in this case are also taught "to obey everything" that Jesus

---

personal but purely historical: Peter was the first of the disciples to confess Jesus as the Christ, or the one who took the lead in the immediate post-Easter church. Catholic interpreters have seen in this verse the granting of primacy in the church to Peter *and* his successors (that is, the popes).

44. Matthew 16:13–19.

45. I take the reference to the "keys" and that to "binding" and "loosing" as indicating that the church, with Peter at its lead, in representing and declaring the "gospel of the kingdom," compels others to decide for or against God's kingdom. This is certainly consistent with what Matthew says elsewhere (compare Matthew 10:11–15, 40; for the idea of "keys" to the "kingdom," see also 23:13). The language of "binding" and "loosing" suggests as well the authority to convey Jesus' teaching and to pronounce on its application to concrete situations as they arise. In Matthew 18:18, "binding" and "loosing" are the prerogatives of all the disciples ("you" here is plural in number) and include responsibility for banishing unrepentant wrongdoers from the community.

46. Matthew 28:19.

47. See Matthew 3:1–12.

commanded his disciples.[48] By being baptized in the name of Father, Son, and Holy Spirit, they indicate their devotion to the God who redeems his people through the work of Jesus Christ (the Son) and by the power of his Spirit.

2. Matthew is content to write of Jesus' last supper with his disciples without mentioning its regular commemoration in the eucharistic meals of the church.[49] Obviously, his first readers were in no need of such a reminder; indeed, the words Matthew uses to describe the original event may well have been part of the service in which it was recalled.

3. The church has its boundaries: those who persist in sin in spite of the warnings they are given are to be excluded.[50] But Matthew does not envisage exclusion happening very often. In the Gospel account, just before Jesus spells out procedures for disciplining the wayward, he reminds his listeners that a shepherd is bound to search for each sheep that goes astray, and declares that God is similarly unwilling that "one of these little ones should be lost."[51] Immediately following the instructions for discipline, Jesus insists that there are to be no limits to the forgiveness his disciples show one another, as God himself is always willing to forgive.[52]

4. The church has its leaders: some must teach,[53] some must carry out the disciplinary procedures Jesus outlines,[54] and so on. But leadership in the church must be exercised in a way consistent with Jesus' teaching: in humble service of others and without any ostentation.

> But you are not to be called rabbi, for you have one teacher, and you are all students. And call no one your father on earth, for you have

Leadership in the church must be exercised in a way consistent with Jesus' teaching: in humble service of others and without any ostentation.

48. Matthew 28:20. The Gospel of Matthew was no doubt meant, in part at least, to serve as a handbook for such instruction.
49. Matthew 26:26–29.
50. The procedures to be followed are outlined in Matthew 18:15–20. They stress the need to give the wrongdoer ample opportunity to repent, with wider attention drawn to the issue only when warnings given more privately are ignored.
51. Matthew 18:12–14.
52. Matthew 18:21–35.
53. Matthew 28:20.
54. Matthew 18:15–20.

one Father—the one in heaven. Nor are you to be called instructors, for you have one instructor, the Messiah. The greatest among you will be your servant. All who exalt themselves will be humbled, and all who humble themselves will be exalted.[55]

5. Disciples of Jesus will naturally be a part of his church; but not all who associate with the church are true disciples of Jesus.[56] Some accept the invitation to the kingdom without altering their lifestyle. Some call Jesus "Lord" but do not obey his commands. Some do mighty works in his name but remain "evildoers."[57] Some are false prophets, "ravenous wolves" disguised in "sheep's clothing."[58] All will be known—and judged—by their "fruits" (that is, the moral caliber of their lives).

> You will know them by their fruits. Are grapes gathered from thorns, or figs from thistles? In the same way, every good tree bears good fruit, but the bad tree bears bad fruit. A good tree cannot bear bad fruit, nor can a bad tree bear good fruit. Every tree that does not bear good fruit is cut down and thrown into the fire. Thus you will know them by their fruits.[59]

For all it says about love, Matthew's Gospel is replete with warnings, like this, of judgment. The new age, after all, is necessarily one of goodness: how can it rise above the self-seeking viciousness of the present age unless its members are those who have delighted in, submitted to, been transformed by, and come to reflect the goodness of the heavenly Father? Divine goodness, Matthew insists, has spared no cost—not even, beyond all comprehension, the cost of the cross of Jesus—to include all creation in its sphere. But not even divine goodness can admit to its realm those who want no part of—divine goodness.[60]

> Not even divine goodness can admit to its realm those who want no part of—divine goodness.

55. Matthew 23:8–12.
56. See the discussion in chapter 5, above, under the heading "The Invitation to God's Kingdom."
57. Matthew 7:22–23.
58. Matthew 7:15.
59. Matthew 7:16–20.
60. In a sermon preached in London in 1933, Bonhoeffer reflected on the claim that *Christ* is humanity's judge: "Christ judges. It is truly serious. But it also means:

Bonhoeffer's *Discipleship*

The Gospel of Matthew is certainly worth studying on its own, but only academics do so. The Gospel comes to us as the first book—the introduction, so to speak—of the Christian "New Testament"; and although, in Christian experience and belief, the voice of God is to be heard in Matthew's Gospel, the same is true of all the other books of the New Testament—and the "Old Testament" too. It follows that the words of God in Matthew's Gospel must be heeded but not isolated from what God says in the rest of the Bible. For the Christian, each part of Scripture must be interpreted together with, and in the light of, every other part of Scripture.

At its best, the interpretation of Scripture through Scripture can be a dynamic, exhilarating exercise. At its worst, the impact and distinctive voice of parts of Scripture gets lost because texts taken from elsewhere in the Bible become the lens through which all Scripture is read. In Bonhoeffer's Lutheran tradition, Matthew's call to discipleship was, Bonhoeffer believed, scarcely to be heard because a distorted reading of texts from Paul's letters had become the basis for (mis)understanding the whole Bible. In the process the message of God's infinitely demanding, infinitely forgiving goodness had been transformed into a proclamation of "cheap grace."

> In Bonhoeffer's Lutheran tradition, Matthew's call to discipleship was scarcely to be heard.

In Paul's own view, humankind—ever since Adam—is hopelessly entangled in a web of sin.[61] Our values, desires, and thinking as well as our deeds show the distortion that inevitably follows when we fail to give God the thanks and obedience God is due. Sinners we are, but loved by God nonetheless; and "God proves his love for us in that while we still were sinners Christ died for us."[62]

---

the Compassionate One judges, he who lived among tax collectors and sinners, who was tempted even as we are, who carried and endured in his own body our sufferings, our fears, our desires, who knows us and calls us by name. Christ judges; that means, grace is the judge, forgiveness, and love. Whoever clings to these is already acquitted" (*A Testament to Freedom: The Essential Writings of Dietrich Bonhoeffer*, ed. Geffrey B. Kelly and F. Burton Nelson [San Francisco: Harper, 1990], 230).

61. See especially Romans 1:18–32; 3:9–20; 5:12–14.

62. Romans 5:8.

Since Christ died for our sins, God can declare even sinners to be righteous (or "justified," as the term is traditionally translated) if they turn in faith to him;[63] he can make of them a new humanity, patterned after Christ and his obedience rather than after Adam, who transgressed.[64]

But humanity's religious instinct, Bonhoeffer wryly observes, is ever on the alert to acquire God's grace at the cheapest possible price.[65] Paul's gospel of grace that declares sinners righteous is easily distorted into an attitude that treats sin as indifferent. Not the sinner but the sin itself is justified. Grace is offered without a change of life, without discipleship, without the cross, without Jesus Christ.

> Humanity's religious instinct, Bonhoeffer wryly observes, is ever on the alert to acquire God's grace at the cheapest possible price.

> Everything remains as before, and I can be sure that God's grace takes care of me. The whole world has become "Christian" under this grace. . . . Christian life [it is claimed] consists of my living in the world and like the world, my not being any different from it, my not being permitted to be different from it—for the sake of grace!—but my going occasionally from the sphere of the world to the sphere of the church, in order to be reassured there of the forgiveness of my sins. I am liberated from following Jesus—by cheap grace, which has to be the bitterest enemy of discipleship.[66]

Properly understood, grace calls us to be disciples of Jesus Christ; properly understood, grace is costly.

> Costly grace is the hidden treasure in the field, for the sake of which people go and sell with joy everything they have. . . . It is the call of Jesus Christ which causes a disciple to leave his nets and follow him. . . . It is costly, because it calls to discipleship; it is grace, because it calls us to follow *Jesus Christ*. It is costly, because it costs people their lives. It is grace, because it thereby makes them live. It is costly, because it condemns sin; it is grace, because it justifies the sinner. Above all, grace is costly, because . . . it costs God the life of God's

63. Romans 3:21–26; 4:5–8; 5:6–11.
64. Romans 5:12–21.
65. Bonhoeffer, *Discipleship* (2001), 49.
66. Ibid., 50–51.

Son. . . . Above all, it is grace because the life of God's Son was not too costly for God to give in order to make us live.[67]

Only those who in following Christ leave everything they have can stand and say that they are justified solely by grace. They recognize the call to discipleship itself as grace and grace as that call. But those who want to use this grace to excuse themselves from discipleship are deceiving themselves.[68]

What is discipleship? Not the disciplined pursuit of an ideal, nor life lived strictly according to a set of principles or laws. Discipleship means adherence to Christ. Because Christ *is* Christ, he must be followed; indeed, only Christ, only the God-man, can call to discipleship.[69] Such a call is not preceded by faith on the part of the one to be called; the call creates the situation in which faith first becomes possible. It is only those who believe who obey Jesus' call; on the other hand, only those who obey the call truly believe.[70] If people "want to learn to believe in God, they have to follow the Son of God incarnate and walk with him."[71]

> It is only those who believe who obey Jesus' call. On the other hand, only those who obey the call truly believe.

The life to which they are called is one whose only security is the company of Jesus Christ. Therein, too, lies its joy.

The disciple is thrown out of the relative security of life into complete insecurity (which in truth is absolute security and protection in community with Jesus); out of the foreseeable and calculable realm (which in truth is unreliable) into the completely unforeseeable, coincidental realm (which in truth is the only necessary and reliable one).[72]

Only Jesus Christ, who bids us follow him, knows where the path will lead. But we know that it will be a path full of mercy beyond measure. Discipleship is joy.[73]

67. Ibid., 44–45.
68. Ibid., 51.
69. Ibid., 59.
70. Ibid., 63.
71. Ibid., 62.
72. Ibid., 58.
73. Ibid., 40.

Jesus calls individuals to follow him; but together they form a new community.

> Everyone enters discipleship alone, but no one remains alone in discipleship. Those who dare to become single individuals trusting in the word are given the gift of church-community.[74]

That community, in Bonhoeffer's day, was gravely threatened.

"Upon This Rock"

In a move designed to silence opposition from the churches, Adolf Hitler announced in mid-July 1933 that church elections would be held on Sunday, July 23.[75] By now the media were firmly under Hitler's control, and with their backing and the help of the Nazi Party, the "German Christians," whose slogan was "Build the new Church of Christ in the new State of Adolf Hitler," were assured victory. Opposition rallies were broken up. Critique of the German Christians was treated as betrayal of the state. In a radio broadcast to the nation on the eve of the election, Hitler made it clear that he expected the results to favor forces "that are exemplified by the German Christians who stand firmly upon the foundation of the Nationalist Socialist [Nazi] State."

Bonhoeffer canceled the lecture he would normally have given during the week prior to the election and set to work preparing leaflets backing opposition candidates. He personally visited Gestapo headquarters to protest the seizing and confiscation of the leaflets. On the day of the election, the results a foregone conclusion, Bonhoeffer preached in Trinity Church in Berlin. His text was Matthew 16:16–18.

In these verses Peter—who is nothing but "a person who has been confronted by Christ and who has recognized Christ"—confesses his faith in Christ; "and this confessing Peter is called the rock on which Christ will build his church."[76] Peter's church, then, is "the church of the confession of Christ";

---

74. Ibid., 99.

75. The following account is based on Eberhard Bethge, *Dietrich Bonhoeffer: A Biography*, rev. ed. (Minneapolis: Fortress, 2000), 291–96.

76. Bonhoeffer, *Testament to Freedom*, 226.

not a church in which what "people say" is talked about but the church
in which Peter's confession is made anew and passed on; the church
which has no other purpose in song, prayer, preaching, and action
than to pass on its confession of faith; the church which is always
founded on rock as long as it remains within these limits, but which
turns into a house built on sand, which is blown away by the wind,
as soon as it is foolhardy enough to think that it may depart from or
even for a moment neglect this purpose.[77]

On the other hand, as the text from Matthew also makes clear,
it is Christ who builds the church. We confess; he builds. Not
knowing his plan, we can never be sure whether at any given
moment he is tearing down or building up. What may seem to
us times of the church's collapse may in fact be times of con-
struction; what strike us as times of the church's prosperity may
in fact be times of demolition. But the task of building can be
left to Christ.

Pay no heed to views and opinions, . . . don't always be calculating
what will happen. . . . Let the church remain the church! But church
confess, confess, confess! Christ alone is your Lord, from his grace
alone can you live as you are. Christ builds.[78]

Against the church the gates of hell—no empty words in Bonhoeffer's day—cannot prevail. The church is eternal because
Christ protects her. Waves pass over her; at times she appears
lost. But

whether the band of believers is great or small, low or high, weak or
strong, if it confesses Christ the victory is assured to them in eter-
nity. . . . The city of God is built on a sure foundation. Amen.[79]

---

77. Ibid., 227.
78. Ibid., 228.
79. Ibid.

8

The Story
of Matthew

Ask ten people what seem to them the ten most important events of the 1990s, and you might end up with a list of a hundred different happenings. For one person, all that matters takes place in the world of politics; for another, in that of sports; for still others, in the world of medicine or the entertainment industry. For many people, the events of real significance are those that mark the progress or setbacks of a cause to which they are committed. What matters greatly to one person may hold little interest for another.

For that matter, what matters greatly to *everyone* may hold little interest for many. Many Europeans in the 1930s, we may assume, paid little heed to political developments. But their lives, too, were forever changed when Hitler became chancellor in Germany.

In the belief of religious Jews, Christians, and Muslims,[1] what matters most to everyone—regardless of our level of interest—is that we are all God's creatures, responsible before God for what

1. That is, what follows represents a conviction common to the Abrahamic (or monotheistic) faiths.

we do with our lives. For the devout Muslim, nature is filled with signs of God's providence meant to provoke people to reflection, gratitude, and submission to God. God has, moreover, sent prophets to remind human beings of their obligations and of the judgment that awaits those who do not fulfill them. Whether humans heed these signs and warnings is their own responsibility. According to Jewish and Christian faith, God is concerned not simply to warn his wayward creatures but also to redeem his creation. Christians believe that God redeems his lost creation through the work of Jesus Christ. Matthew, who shares the latter conviction, tells us Jesus' story.

> In the belief of religious Jews, Christians, and Muslims, what matters most is that we are all God's creatures, responsible before God for what we do with our lives.

What remains curious about the Gospel is that Matthew is content *simply* to tell a story. For reasons that should by now be evident, what matters most for Matthew is that people acknowledge Jesus as God's Messiah, be baptized as his disciples, and obey his teaching. These convictions undoubtedly formed the substance of many sermons Matthew heard—perhaps of many he himself delivered. But Matthew's Gospel is not a sermon, and (here at least) Matthew does not preach. At no point in the Gospel does he directly address his readers with a call for belief or obedience. Rather he simply relates that at a particular point in Jesus' career and in a particular place, Peter burst out with the words "You are the Messiah, the Son of the Living God"; that Jesus, before leaving his disciples, gave them instructions to baptize others; that at various points in their lives together Jesus told his disciples how *they* ought to live. From these stories of the past, readers are left to draw their own conclusions.

> What matters most for Matthew is that people acknowledge Jesus as God's Messiah, be baptized as his disciples, and obey his teaching. But Matthew's Gospel is not a sermon, and Matthew does not preach.

Part of Matthew's reason for leaving things as he did may simply have been that he knew who his initial readers would be; he knew that they were already convinced that Jesus is the

Messiah, and that they had already been baptized and instructed in Jesus' teaching. They already knew, too, the stories Matthew recounts; probably they had heard more than a few sermons that took these stories as their base. Matthew was not writing to inform the ignorant or persuade the skeptical. He was simply providing believers with a readily accessible and more permanent form of traditions with which they were already familiar.

This may be part, but it cannot be the whole, of the explanation why Matthew tells of the past without speaking directly to the present. After all, no reader of Matthew's Gospel can confuse it with a random collection of notes, with raw material thought to be digestible only when it has been cooked up into a sermon. On the contrary, the Gospel is clearly meant to stand on its own. It reads, in some ways at least, no differently than any other story, advancing from a clear introduction through a developing plot to what is unmistakably its conclusion. If Matthew chooses not to supplement his telling of the past with an application for the present, he must be convinced that what matters most can be conveyed simply by telling a story—provided, of course, that the story is that of Jesus.

> Matthew believes that the eternal God was "with us" in the Jesus who lived in the past. It follows that the choices people faced when they encountered Jesus are, in effect, the perennial choices people must make for or against God.

On one level, the story of Jesus belongs to the unrepeatable past. "In the time of King Herod," Jesus was born in Bethlehem.[2] It could not have been otherwise, since a divine script was being followed: "All this took place to fulfill what had been spoken by the Lord through the prophet."[3] The same, Matthew believes, could be said of everything that happened in the course of Jesus' life. Above all, Jesus' death and resurrection were one-time events at the turning point of history: God's goodness then triumphed decisively over all the powers of darkness.

But Matthew also believes that the eternal God was "with us" in the Jesus who lived in the past.[4] It follows that the choices

---

2. Matthew 2:1.
3. Matthew 1:22; see also, for example, 2:3–6, 15, 17–18.
4. Matthew 1:23.

people faced when they encountered Jesus are, in effect, the perennial choices people must make for or against God. The demands Jesus made of his contemporaries are the eternal demands of God. The power that Jesus displayed for the good of his contemporaries was the power of God—and it remains available to all who call on him. Matthew writes, then, in the conviction that alert readers will sense at once that they, too, are addressed when Jesus in Matthew 4 summons Simon and Andrew, James and John to follow him; that they, too, face the choice of the wealthy young man of Matthew 19 whether to follow Jesus or cling to their possessions; that they, like Peter in Matthew 18, are being told to forgive without limitations; that they, like the disciples in Matthew 8 and 14, are secure with Jesus in the midst of a storm. Christ is ever our contemporary.

Enough for Matthew, then, to tell his story. In the midst of their own very diverse situations, readers cannot fail to hear afresh, in the words of the Gospel, the call of God: the invitation to God's kingdom, the summons to follow Jesus.

Many parts of this story have already been touched upon in earlier chapters. That the Gospel *is* a story may, however, be forgotten if we simply focus on its themes. It is fitting that we conclude with a look at the *story* of Matthew's Gospel.

Introducing the Characters

For those with eyes to see, God is at work in the course of history: so Matthew affirms from the first verse of his Gospel. His very first words—literally, "The book of the *genesis* of Jesus Christ," where *genesis* may mean "origin, birth," or perhaps "family tree, genealogy," or even "history"—are ambiguous but more important for what they echo than for what they say. Genesis is, after all, the title of the first book of the Bible.[5] The *sacred* history that begins in Genesis, Matthew is suggesting, continues with the story of "Jesus the Messiah, the son of David, the son of Abraham."

5. The phrase "book of the *genesis*," with which Matthew begins his Gospel, is found in the Greek version of Genesis 2:4 (literally, "This is the book of the origin [*genesis*] of heaven and earth") and Genesis 5:1 (literally, "This is the book of the origin [*genesis*] of human beings").

Every human being has a family tree. Every Jew, it was thought, could, in principle at least, trace his or her family tree to Abraham; some Jews could trace it to David as well. Matthew might appear, then, to use the opening verses of his Gospel to pass on, for our information, the names of Jesus' ancestors and, for our curiosity, the singular observation that the same number of generations (fourteen) lay between Abraham and David as between David and the Babylonian exile and between the Babylonian exile and the birth of Jesus.[6] But sacred history has little time for simple information or curious observations: more is at stake in Matthew's genealogy than meets the eye. With the names of Jesus' (male) ancestors, Matthew includes the names of women whose non-Jewish connections perhaps suggest that God intends to number Gentiles among his people and whose unconventional, or even unseemly, entrance into relations with an ancestor of Jesus perhaps anticipates the offense that surrounded Jesus' own birth.[7] The emphasis on Abraham, David, and the Babylonian exile in Jesus' genealogy suggests the unfolding of a divine history that culminates in the coming of the Messiah.[8] The repeated intervals of fourteen generations represent Matthew's way of saying that the story of Jesus, like those of Abraham, David, and the Babylonian exile, marks a turning point in the history of God's people.[9]

> For Matthew, the *sacred* history that begins in Genesis continues with the story of Jesus.

The wonder of God's entrance into human history is signaled by the wonder of Jesus' birth:

6. "So all the generations from Abraham to David are fourteen generations; and from David to the deportation to Babylon, fourteen generations; and from the deportation to Babylon to the Messiah, fourteen generations" (Matthew 1:17).

7. Tamar gave birth to twins through relations with her father-in-law Judah (Genesis 38:1–30). Before her relations with Salmon, Rahab was a Canaanite prostitute (Joshua 2:1). Ruth was a Moabite with an extraordinary love story (the book of Ruth). Bathsheba became David's wife to regularize an adulterous relationship after David contrived the death of her first husband (2 Samuel 11:1–27).

8. See chapter 4, above.

9. That the fourteen generations represent not a curiosity that Matthew observes but a pattern that he imposes to make a point is apparent, for example, when one compares 1 Chronicles 3:11–12 with Matthew 1:8–9: between Joram and Jotham, Chronicles lists four generations, Matthew one. The Gospel writer thus abbreviates the list by three to make his point.

When his mother Mary had been engaged to Joseph, but before they lived together, she was found to be with child from the Holy Spirit.[10]

Joseph subsequently acts on behalf of "the child and his mother,"[11] but he has no role in the child's conception. Yet even in his conception Jesus compels a response of faith or offense: Mary is pregnant, but she has not yet entered Joseph's home as his wife. Joseph, knowing that he has not impregnated her, draws the natural conclusion, although, "being a righteous man and unwilling to expose her to public disgrace," he plans "to dismiss her quietly."[12] A word from the Lord creates the occasion for faith:

> But just when he had resolved to do this, an angel of the Lord appeared to him in a dream and said, "Joseph, son of David, do not be afraid to take Mary as your wife, for the child conceived in her is from the Holy Spirit. She will bear a son, and you are to name him Jesus, for he will save his people from their sins."[13]

Joseph believes and obeys the angel's words. And all the while, beyond the horizons of the actors who choose the role of faith or unbelief, the divinely scripted drama is unfolding:

> All this took place to fulfill what had been spoken by the Lord through the prophet.[14]

Jesus' birth, too, elicits both faith and unbelief: faith from unexpected quarters, unbelief from those more closely concerned. A star signaling the birth of the "king of the Jews" draws "wise men from the East" first to Jerusalem, then to Bethlehem to see the child; "overwhelmed with joy," they bring him worship and costly gifts.[15] The same news awakens in "King Herod" and "all Jerusalem with him" no curiosity, no wonder, and certainly no openness to the divinely promised, divinely signaled initiative;

10. Matthew 1:18.
11. Matthew 2:13–14, 20–21. See also 2:11.
12. Matthew 1:19.
13. Matthew 1:20–21.
14. Matthew 1:22.
15. Matthew 2:1–11.

only great distress.[16] No effort is made on their part to see the child, but Herod—like Pharaoh centuries before him—does what he can to destroy a perceived threat.[17] And still, as players choose their parts, the scripted drama unfolds.[18]

After the stories of Jesus' infancy, Matthew turns our attention to John, called "the Baptist" because of his striking practice of immersing in the Jordan River those who come to him "confessing their sins."[19] The confession and the baptism are both in response to John's call in the desert for people to repent and prepare for God's kingdom.

> The wonder of God's entrance into human history is signaled by the wonder of Jesus' birth. Yet even in his birth Jesus compels a response of faith or offense.

> In those days John the Baptist appeared in the wilderness of Judea, proclaiming, "Repent, for the kingdom of heaven has come near."[20]

Clearly, Matthew has cast John's essential message as identical to that of Jesus;[21] indeed, Matthew sees John as Jesus' forerunner, whose own role, like that of Jesus, was forecast in Scripture.

> This is the one of whom the prophet Isaiah spoke when he said,
>   "The voice of one crying out in the wilderness:
>   'Prepare the way of the Lord,
>   make his paths straight.'"[22]

John's message, as conveyed by Matthew, focuses on the outpouring of divine judgment that awaits those unfit for a place in God's kingdom. Religious leaders, no less than others, need to repent if they are to escape the "wrath to come."[23] Descent from Abraham provides no exemption from judgment: "God is

---

16. Matthew 2:3.
17. Matthew 2:16. Compare Exodus 1:8–2:15. See the discussion in chapter 4, above, under the heading "Moses."
18. Matthew 2:5–6, 15, 17–18, 23.
19. Matthew 3:1–6.
20. Matthew 3:1–2.
21. Compare Matthew 4:17.
22. Matthew 3:3. The quotation is taken from Isaiah 40:3.
23. Matthew 3:7–8.

able from these stones to raise up children to Abraham."[24] What is required, John insists, is "good fruit" (appropriate conduct) in people's lives if they are not to be cut down like trees put to the ax.[25]

Jesus himself comes to John to be baptized. Not that Jesus has committed sins for which he needs forgiveness. But John is a messenger divinely commissioned, and Jesus begins his public career with an act of humility and submission to God, aligning himself with God's prophet. And God responds by acknowledging his Son. Subsequent stories of human opposition to Jesus are thus seen from the start as disloyalty to God.

> Jesus begins his public career with an act of humility and submission to God, aligning himself with God's prophet. And God responds by acknowledging his Son.

And when Jesus had been baptized, just as he came up from the water, suddenly the heavens were opened to him and he saw the Spirit of God descending like a dove and alighting on him. And a voice from heaven said, "This is my Son, the Beloved, with whom I am well pleased."[26]

Before launching his public activities, however, Jesus is tempted by Satan: this, too, is part of the divine plan, the devil himself now its unwitting executor.[27] In the future, Jesus will miraculously provide bread for crowds of people;[28] but he rejects the temptation to do so for himself, choosing rather to live in dependence on God.[29] He will one day use God's power to do many "mighty works" for others; but he refuses to attract attention to himself with a display of power for its own sake.[30] After submitting, in life as well as in death, to his Father's will, he will be given "all authority in heaven and on earth";[31] but power for

---

24. Matthew 3:9.
25. Matthew 3:10.
26. Matthew 3:16–17.
27. "Then Jesus was *led up by the Spirit* into the wilderness *to be tempted by the devil*" (Matthew 4:1).
28. Matthew 14:13–21; 15:32–38.
29. Matthew 4:2–4.
30. Matthew 4:5–7.
31. Matthew 28:18.

its own sake he refuses to grasp.[32] In every respect Jesus proves himself a faithful Son.

Lines Are Drawn

When John is arrested, both prudence and the divine script require that Jesus withdraw to Galilee.[33] Making his home in "Capernaum by the sea," he begins to proclaim, as John the Baptist had proclaimed, "Repent, for the kingdom of heaven has come near."[34] Simon and Andrew, James and John are summoned to follow Jesus; they obey. Jesus goes "throughout Galilee, teaching in their synagogues and proclaiming the good news of the kingdom and curing every disease and every sickness among the people."[35]

At this point Matthew introduces the Sermon on the Mount—the most famous chapters in his Gospel, and among the best known texts in all of literature—in which he has collected traditions of Jesus' ethical teaching.[36] That Matthew believes Jesus' words should be practiced by all his readers is obvious,[37] but in his Gospel they form an integral part of his story. Jesus speaks his "sermon" on a mountain to disciples gathered around him.[38] The crowds who listen are astounded[39]—although astonishment, we may note, is not the same as discipleship.

The miracle stories that follow in Matthew 8 and 9 are summed up by Jesus himself in Matthew 11 when he responds to messengers from John:

Go and tell John what you hear and see: the blind receive their sight, the lame walk, the lepers are cleansed, the deaf hear, the dead are

32. Matthew 4:8–10.
33. Matthew 4:12–16.
34. Matthew 4:17. See the discussion in chapter 5, above, under the heading "The Invitation to God's Kingdom."
35. Matthew 4:23.
36. See the discussion in chapters 2, 3, and 7, above.
37. See Matthew 7:24–27; 28:19–20.
38. Matthew 5:1–2.
39. Matthew 7:28–29.

raised, and the poor have good news brought to them. And blessed is anyone who takes no offense at me.[40]

Interpreted correctly, then, Jesus' works of power are signs that Jesus is "the one who [according to the divine script] is to come" and that with him the kingdom of God is dawning.[41] Where God is at work, people take sides.[42] Matthew 8 and 9 show God at work not simply in the miracles of Jesus but also in the forgiveness of sins that Jesus pronounces in word[43] and enacts in deed by keeping company with "sinners."[44] In response to the divine activity, the needy come to Jesus in faith and find help. On the other hand, some, though interested, are not prepared to pay the price to be Jesus' disciples.[45] The disciples themselves have their moments of doubt.[46] And naysayers and critics abound: Jesus, they remark, presumes on the prerogatives of God when he forgives sins; the disreputable company he keeps discredits his message; his followers lack the solemnity required of the religious; and Jesus' miraculous powers must come from the devil.[47] Early in the Gospel, lines are being drawn.

> Interpreted correctly, Jesus' works of power are signs that Jesus is "the one who is to come" and that with him the kingdom of God is dawning.

To expand his outreach, Jesus commissions his disciples to "go . . . to the lost sheep of the house of Israel," bringing them Jesus' message of the kingdom, repeating in their midst Jesus' works of power—and anticipating the hostility to which Jesus himself is subject.[48] For his part, Jesus decries the indifference

40. Matthew 11:4–6. On the nature of the "offense," see the discussion in chapter 5, above, under the heading "The Invitation to God's Kingdom."

41. Matthew 11:3; 12:28.

42. See chapter 6, above.

43. Matthew 9:2.

44. Matthew 9:10–13.

45. Matthew 8:18–22.

46. Matthew 8:23–27.

47. Matthew 9:2–3, 11, 14, 34. Remarkably, both the asceticism of John and the conviviality of Jesus betoken the approach of God's kingdom (John, the seriousness of pending judgment; Jesus, the joys of God's children); predictably, both are subjected to critique (see Matthew 11:16–19).

48. Matthew 10:1–42.

of the Galilean cities toward his activities but continues to extend an invitation to all who are "weary and are carrying heavy burdens" to come to him for rest.[49]

By the time we reach Matthew 12, we have seen God acknowledge Jesus[50] and angels serve him;[51] leprosy, fever (and every other sickness and disease), the winds, the sea, demons, and death itself have all complied with Jesus' words.[52] Human beings, on the other hand, are by no means so compliant, and Matthew 12 shows how some carp over his apparent disregard of the Sabbath and repeat the charge that he derives power from a pact with the devil. As Matthew presents things, Jesus does not so much disregard the Sabbath as prioritize human need over its scrupulous observance—for which, he points out, there is precedent both in Scripture and in universal practice.[53] The charge of working with the devil Jesus dismisses by noting that the devil is in fact the object of his attacks, the oppressor from whose power he delivers; and he warns that although for every other sin there is forgiveness, there can be none for people who blaspheme (as those who raise *this* charge have just blasphemed) the work of God's Spirit.[54] In a similar vein he dismisses the contempt for his mission that veils itself in a request for a "sign" to prove his legitimacy.[55]

> The parables Jesus speaks serve to stimulate the thinking and provoke the insight of those prepared to listen, but they strike the closed-minded as trite and unilluminating.

Jesus' listeners, it appears, are divided into those who "have" hearts open to receive his message and those who decidedly do not.[56] In Matthew 13 Jesus adopts a mode of communication suited to both types:[57] the parables he speaks serve to stimulate the thinking and provoke the insight of those prepared to listen;

---

49. Matthew 11:20–30.
50. Matthew 3:17.
51. Matthew 4:11.
52. Matthew 4:23; 8:3, 14–15, 27, 31–32; 9:18–26.
53. Matthew 12:1–13.
54. Matthew 12:22–32.
55. Matthew 12:38–42.
56. Matthew 13:12.
57. Matthew 13:10–17.

at the same time they can only strike the closed-minded as trite and unilluminating. The kingdom of heaven is like a farmer sowing seed on different types of soil; or like a tiny seed destined to grow into a great shrub; or like a treasure hidden in a field, or a pearl of great price.[58] "Let anyone with ears listen!"[59]

Manifest Destiny

The story pauses briefly in Matthew 14 as Matthew provides background information. John the Baptist gained Herod's attention by rebuking him for living with Herodias, his brother Philip's wife.[60] Herod arrests John but deems it imprudent to kill him: too many of his subjects believe that John is a prophet. Herodias's daughter dances for Herod and his guests on Herod's birthday. Herod, enchanted, promises to give her whatever she asks. She consults her mother, then requests John's head. Herod obliges her. Jesus, hearing the report, withdraws to a desert place.

But crowds still gather. When they remain in his company until late in the day, Jesus takes on the role of their host, giving them all they can eat from the "five loaves and two fish" that are available:[61] a story that, looking back, recalls how God miraculously fed the ancient Israelites in the wilderness[62] and, looking ahead, anticipates the banquet of the blessed in the kingdom of heaven.[63] The aura of God's presence is even more unmistakable when Jesus approaches his disciples' boat at night, walking on the water; he comforts them with the words "Take heart, I am; do not be afraid";[64] and he causes the wind to cease.[65] Not other-

58. See the discussion in chapter 5, above, under the heading "The Invitation to God's Kingdom."

59. Matthew 13:9.

60. The Herod here is Herod Antipas, the son of the Herod who figured in the stories of Jesus' birth and infancy (Matthew 2).

61. Matthew 14:13–21.

62. See, in particular, Exodus 16.

63. Matthew 8:11.

64. Matthew 14:27, translated literally; the NRSV reads, "It is I," for the Greek "I am." The words in Greek recall the divine name of Exodus 3:14.

65. That God calms the sea and rescues those threatened by its waves is the theme of Psalm 107:23–32.

wise known for their perspicacity, the disciples this time exclaim, "Truly you are the Son of God."[66]

The carping continues ("Why do your disciples break the tradition of the elders? For they do not wash their hands before they eat.").[67] So do accounts of healing, of a miraculous meal, of contemptuous demands from Jesus' foes for a sign of his legitimation, of monumental obtuseness on the part of Jesus' disciples.[68] But just when we think this could go on forever, Jesus declares that it cannot.

> The aura of God's presence is unmistakable when Jesus approaches his disciples' boat at night, walking on the water; he comforts them with the words "Take heart, I am; do not be afraid."

He elicits from his disciples popular opinion of who he is, then puts to them this question:

"But who do you say that I am?" Simon Peter answered, "You are the Messiah, the Son of the living God." And Jesus answered him, "Blessed are you, Simon son of Jonah! For flesh and blood has not revealed this to you, but my Father in heaven."[69]

Messiah he is; but the path laid out for the Messiah is not what they anticipate.

From that time on, Jesus began to show his disciples that he must go to Jerusalem and undergo great suffering at the hands of the elders and chief priests and scribes, and be killed, and on the third day be raised.[70]

Indeed, those who would follow Jesus must take up a cross of their own.[71]

At this point, and for one brief shining moment, Jesus appears to his closest disciples in heavenly splendor—on a high mountain with Moses and Elijah. Once again he is acknowledged by God with a voice from a cloud; the voice overwhelms the disciples and drives them to the ground.

66. Matthew 14:33.
67. Matthew 15:2.
68. Matthew 15:21–16:12.
69. Matthew 16:15–17.
70. Matthew 16:21.
71. Matthew 16:24.

This is my Son, the Beloved; with him I am well pleased; listen to him!

When the disciples pick themselves up, the cloud, the heavenly visitors, and the glory are gone.[72] The clarity granted in a moment of revelation must sustain them through the darkness and doubts that lie ahead.

> For one brief shining moment, Jesus appears to his closest disciples in heavenly splendor. The clarity granted in a moment of revelation must sustain them through the darkness and doubts that lie ahead.

Jesus and his disciples head toward Jerusalem. The occasional miracle story is still related.[73] We are told of a single debate ("Is it lawful for a man to divorce his wife for any cause?").[74] And there is some interaction with the omnipresent crowds.[75] But most of what we read now concerns Jesus' instruction of his disciples: the need for faith in prayer[76] and for humility to enter God's kingdom;[77] how to treat a wayward brother and the importance of forgiveness;[78] the perils of wealth and the rewards of those who abandon what they have to follow Jesus;[79] God's unstinting generosity and the path to greatness through service.[80] Repeatedly, too, we are reminded of what Jerusalem will bring.[81] Jesus' death will neither follow nor interrupt the completion of his mission; it is itself his mission's goal.

> Jesus' death neither follows nor interrupts the completion of his mission; it is itself his mission's goal.

Jesus' entrance into Jerusalem[82] is carefully staged so that it corresponds precisely

---

72. Matthew 17:1–8.
73. Matthew 17:14–18, 24–27; 20:29–34.
74. Matthew 19:3–9, with follow-up discussion in 19:10–12.
75. Matthew 19:13–15. Perhaps a wider audience is assumed for the parable of 20:1–16 as well, since immediately after it is told (20:17), Jesus draws aside his disciples to speak to them privately.
76. Matthew 17:19–20; see also 21:18–22.
77. Matthew 18:1–5.
78. Matthew 18:12–35.
79. Matthew 19:16–30.
80. Matthew 20:1–16, 20–28.
81. Matthew 17:12, 22–23; 20:17–19, 22, 28.
82. Matthew 21:1–11.

to the divine script;[83] as he enters the city, Jerusalem is, in effect, invited to recognize its messianic king. The script then calls for Jesus to enter the temple courtyard and drive from the sacred precincts those who have transformed them into a marketplace.[84] Recognizing that a gauntlet has been thrown down, the "chief priests and the elders of the people" approach Jesus and demand to know who gave him the right to "do these things." Jesus responds by testing their willingness to acknowledge the divine commission behind John's call for repentance. The issue he raises is a sensitive one. At the time, Jesus' interlocutors had ignored John's call, so they can hardly now concede John's commission; yet they prefer not to antagonize the public by denying it. When they cannot say who authorized John, Jesus refuses to speak of his own authorization.[85]

Or—to put it more accurately—he gives no *direct* answer to the question of his authority. But the point of the parables that follow could hardly be clearer.[86] It is to the joys of *God's* kingdom that Jesus invites all who hear him; and it is with *God's* judgment that he threatens the corrupt leaders of God's people.

Debates follow: whether taxes should be paid to Caesar, whether the dead will rise again, which commandment is the greatest.[87] Each of the discussions has its own interest; but each is introduced as a challenge to Jesus, and together they signal the hostility felt toward Jesus by Jerusalem's religious establishment. For his part, Jesus proceeds to warn his followers[88] against imitating those who play the game of religion only to shield themselves—and steer others away—from the genuine demands of God.[89] Such people live for the prestige of religious

83. "This took place to fulfill what had been spoken through the prophet, saying, 'Tell the daughter of Zion, Look, your king is coming to you, humble, and mounted on a donkey, and on a colt, the foal of a donkey'" (Matthew 21:4–5, citing Zechariah 9:9).

84. Matthew 21:12–13. The action recalls the words of Zechariah 14:21 and Malachi 3:1–3; Jesus' words on the occasion take up Isaiah 56:7 and Jeremiah 7:11.

85. Matthew 21:23–27.

86. Matthew 21:28–22:14.

87. Matthew 22:15–40.

88. That Jesus warns his followers (and Matthew his readers) of these failings indicates that they are not peculiar to any one religious group; rather they represent the insidious but human tendency to make even service of God a forum for self-promotion.

89. Matthew 23:13–15, 23–26.

leadership and make of their piety a public display. They delight in multiplying burdens to be borne by the faithful and endlessly refine the limits of acceptable compromises with evil.[90] Religion as game calls for careful tithing of every herb on one's table while paying little heed to requirements of justice, mercy, and faith.[91] It makes a spectacle of honoring the memory of prophets whose mouths have long since been silenced but persecutes those who still speak. Jesus' indictment ends with a lament for Jerusalem, the city that houses God's temple but rejects God's messengers: temple and city will soon be left desolate.[92] The end is coming; but before it arrives, hard times await Jesus' disciples. They, too, are forewarned and urged to remain faithful.[93]

> Jesus warns his followers against imitating those who play the game of religion only to shield themselves—and steer others away—from the genuine demands of God.

His teaching finished, Jesus prepares to eat Passover with his disciples. Before the celebration of the meal, a woman shows her devotion by pouring on Jesus' head perfume that cost her a fortune, while a disciple accepts a paltry sum to betray him.[94] During the meal itself, Jesus distributes bread and passes a cup of wine to his disciples, telling them to see in the bread his body, and in the cup his blood, willingly sacrificed to procure their forgiveness.[95] In a place called Gethsemane, Jesus' closest disciples sleep while Jesus prays that, if possible, he may escape the death that awaits him; but "your [God's] will be done."[96] Jesus is arrested, tried, condemned, abused, mocked, and crucified. In the meantime, the disciples abandon him, Peter denies his acquaintance, and Judas, his betrayer, hangs himself.[97]

---

90. In the example Jesus gives, misplaced energy is devoted to distinguishing acceptable formulas for swearing oaths from unacceptable ones (Matthew 23:16–22). Compare Matthew 5:33–37.

91. Matthew 23:23–24.

92. Matthew 23:37–38.

93. Matthew 24:1–25:46. See the discussion in chapter 5, above, under the heading "The Course of God's Kingdom."

94. Matthew 26:1–16.

95. Matthew 26:26–28.

96. Matthew 26:36–45.

97. Matthew 26:47–27:56. See also the discussion in chapter 5, above, under the heading "The Cross and the Kingdom."

Sabbath comes and goes. On the first day of the week, and recalling the angelic announcement of Jesus' birth in Matthew's first chapter, an angel appears in Matthew's final chapter to announce his resurrection. The resurrected Jesus shows himself to the women who saw the angel at his tomb; he instructs them to tell his disciples where to meet him.[98] Those who plotted Jesus' death now plot to explain away his resurrection.[99] But Jesus comes to his disciples and gives them the command that Matthew believes defines the age in which all his readers live:

> All authority in heaven and on earth has been given to me. Go therefore and make disciples of all nations, baptizing them in the name of the Father and of the Son and of the Holy Spirit, and teaching them to obey everything that I have commanded you. And remember, I am with you always, to the end of the age.[100]

∽∾

In August 1944, Dietrich Bonhoeffer sent a birthday greeting from his prison cell to Eberhard Bethge. In it he wrote:

> In these turbulent times we repeatedly lose sight of what really makes life worth living. We think that, because this or that person is living, it makes sense for us to live too. But the truth is that if this earth was good enough for the man Jesus Christ, if such a man as Jesus lived, then, and only then, has life a meaning for us.[101]

"If such a man as Jesus lived, then, and only then, has life a meaning for us."

Bonhoeffer lived nearly two millennia after the Gospel of Matthew was written, but in essential respects he shared its vision for life. If our world is an accident, if we too are an accident, and if our well-being is dependent on the whim of ruthless human beings (as it must have seemed to many in Nazi prisons), then we may well wonder what purpose there is in living. For Matthew as for Bonhoeffer, however, our world is

---

98. Matthew 28:9–10.
99. Matthew 28:11–15.
100. Matthew 28:18–20.
101. Dietrich Bonhoeffer, *Letters and Papers from Prison*, ed. Eberhard Bethge, expanded ed. (New York: Simon & Schuster, 1997), 391.

God's world, and human beings are the objects of God's infinite love; moreover, in the person and activities of Jesus, God was at work in our world, reaffirming its goodness, reclaiming it *for* goodness. It follows that life in the world in which Jesus lived, and even suffering in the world in which Jesus suffered, must be worthwhile. Bonhoeffer showed his grasp of Matthew's story when, a few weeks after his arrest in April 1943, he wrote to his parents:

> At last the tenth day has come round, and I'm allowed to write to you again; I'm so glad to let you know that even here I'm having a happy Easter. Good Friday and Easter free us to think about other things far beyond our own personal fate, about the ultimate meaning of all life, suffering, and events; and we lay hold of a great hope.[102]

102. Ibid., 25.

Index

Abraham, 63–67
alms, 124–25

Babylon, exile in, 74–79
baptism, 133–34
benevolence, God's, 27–29, 37–39,
  129–32. *See also* goodness, God's;
  rule, God's; suffering
blessings. *See* gifts, nature of
Bonhoeffer, Dietrich
  on demons, 90n40
  Discipleship, 8–9, 136–39
  German Christianity and, 7–9,
    139–40
  on God's call, 111n19, 128n31
  on God's goodness, 41–45, 157–58
  on marriage, 54n18
  on prayer, 127n26
  on resurrection, 103n109
  on sin and guilt, 55–59
  on the Trinity, 117n59

charity, 124–25
cheap grace, 136–38
children of God, 115–16
choices, worldviews and, 23
Christ, the, 72–73, 114–15, 142–43
church, the, 7–9, 132–36, 139–40
coherence, worldviews and, 23–24
communication, nature of, 11–13
consistency, worldviews and, 23
creeds, early Christian, 116–17

cross, the, 97–103. *See also* demands,
  Jesus'; suffering

David, 71–74
demands, Jesus', 47–55, 58–59,
  105–8, 110–13, 127–29. *See also*
  invitation, God's
demons, 90n40
deprivation. *See* suffering
Discipleship (Bonhoeffer), 8–9,
  136–39
discipline, church, 134
divinity, Jesus', 110–19

Easter, 103n109
eschatology, the kingdom and, 93–97
Eucharist, the, 134
evil, problem of, 81–82, 90–93
excommunication, 134
exile, Babylonian, 74–79
experience, worldviews and, 22–23

faith, 37–39. *See also* benevolence,
  God's; goodness, God's; invitation,
  God's
fatherhood, God's, 113–17
forgiveness, God's, 54–55, 83, 88–89
fruits, discipleship and, 135

Gentiles, the gospel and, 64–66, 82
gifts, nature of, 34–37
goodness, God's
  evil and, 122–24

159